Racial Nationalisms

This book addresses the centrality of race and racism in consolidating the nationalisms currently prominent in Brexit Britain. Particular attention is given to the issues of refugees, borders and bordering, and the wider forms of nativist and anti-Muslim sentiments that anchor today's increasingly populist forms of nationalist politics. It is argued that the forms of scapegoating and alarmism integral to the revival of nationalism in British politics are fundamentally tied to racialised processes. Equally however, it is argued that such a political climate is not simply discursive, but also yields acute forms of governance, wherein an increasingly violent attention is given by the state to the border. The chapters in the book do however also attempt to think through the possibilities of a constructive response to this moment. Emphasis is given here to the everyday cultural textures that might help shape a popular opposition to racial nationalism. Similarly, the book attempts to unpack the appeal of today's distinctive populism in ways that might be more responsive to anti-racist and anti-nationalist sentiments.

Racial Nationalisms will be of interest to academics and researchers studying postcolonialism, nationalism, ethnic and racial studies, and to advanced students of sociology, political science and public policy.

This book was originally published as a special issue of the journal *Ethnic and Racial Studies*.

Sivamohan Valluvan is Assistant Professor of Sociology at the University of Warwick, UK. His book *The Clamour of Nationalism* was published in 2019.

Virinder S. Kalra is Professor of Sociology at the University of Warwick, UK. He is the author of multiple monographs, including *Beyond Religion in India and Pakistan* (co-authored with Tej Purewal, 2019) and *Sacred and Secular Musics* (2016).

Ethnic and Racial Studies
Series editors: Martin Bulmer, *University of Surrey, UK*, and John Solomos, *University of Warwick, UK*

The journal *Ethnic and Racial Studies* was founded in 1978 by John Stone to provide an international forum for high quality research on race, ethnicity, nationalism and ethnic conflict. At the time the study of race and ethnicity was still a relatively marginal sub-field of sociology, anthropology and political science. In the intervening period the journal has provided a space for the discussion of core theoretical issues, key developments and trends, and for the dissemination of the latest empirical research.

It is now the leading journal in its field and has helped to shape the development of scholarly research agendas. *Ethnic and Racial Studies* attracts submissions from scholars in a diverse range of countries and fields of scholarship, and crosses disciplinary boundaries. It is now available in both printed and electronic form. Since 2015 it has published 15 issues per year, three of which are dedicated to *Ethnic and Racial Studies Review* offering expert guidance to the latest research through the publication of book reviews, symposia and discussion pieces, including reviews of work in languages other than English.

The *Ethnic and Racial Studies* book series contains a wide range of the journal's special issues. These special issues are an important contribution to the work of the journal, where leading social science academics bring together articles on specific themes and issues that are linked to the broad intellectual concerns of *Ethnic and Racial Studies*. The series editors work closely with the guest editors of the special issues to ensure that they meet the highest quality standards possible. Through publishing these special issues as a series of books, we hope to allow a wider audience of both scholars and students from across the social science disciplines to engage with the work of *Ethnic and Racial Studies*.

Most recent titles in the series include:

Everyday Multiculturalism in/across Asia
Edited by Jessica Walton, Anita Harris and Koichi Iwabuchi

Racial Nationalisms
Borders, Refugees and the Cultural Politics of Belonging
Edited by Sivamohan Valluvan and Virinder S. Kalra

Racial Nationalisms
Borders, Refugees and the Cultural Politics of Belonging

Edited by
**Sivamohan Valluvan and
Virinder S. Kalra**

First published 2021
by Routledge
2 Park Square, Milton Park, Abingdon, Oxon OX14 4RN

and by Routledge
52 Vanderbilt Avenue, New York, NY 10017

Routledge is an imprint of the Taylor & Francis Group, an informa business

Chapters 1–2 and 4–6 © 2021 Taylor & Francis
Chapter 3 © 2019 Madeline-Sophie Abbas. Originally published as Open Access.

With the exception of Chapter 3, no part of this book may be reprinted or reproduced or utilised in any form or by any electronic, mechanical, or other means, now known or hereafter invented, including photocopying and recording, or in any information storage or retrieval system, without permission in writing from the publishers. For details on the rights for Chapter 3, please see the chapter's Open Access footnote.

Trademark notice: Product or corporate names may be trademarks or registered trademarks, and are used only for identification and explanation without intent to infringe.

British Library Cataloguing in Publication Data
A catalogue record for this book is available from the British Library

ISBN 13: 978-0-367-56378-3

Typeset in Myriad Pro
by Newgen Publishing UK

Publisher's Note
The publisher accepts responsibility for any inconsistencies that may have arisen during the conversion of this book from journal articles to book chapters, namely the inclusion of journal terminology.

Disclaimer
Every effort has been made to contact copyright holders for their permission to reprint material in this book. The publishers would be grateful to hear from any copyright holder who is not here acknowledged and will undertake to rectify any errors or omissions in future editions of this book.

Contents

	Citation Information	vi
	Notes on Contributors	viii
	Introduction	1
	Sivamohan Valluvan and Virinder S. Kalra	
1	Deportation, racism and multi-status Britain: immigration control and the production of race in the present	21
	Luke de Noronha	
2	More in common: the domestication of misogynist white supremacy and the assassination of Jo Cox	39
	Hannah Jones	
3	Conflating the Muslim refugee and the terror suspect: responses to the Syrian refugee "crisis" in Brexit Britain	58
	Madeline-Sophie Abbas	
4	Care and cruelty in Chios: the "refugee crisis" and the limits of Europe	78
	Malcolm James	
5	Racism and Brexit: notes towards an antiracist populism	98
	Ben Pitcher	
6	"I feel English as fuck": translocality and the performance of alternative identities through rap	118
	Richard Bramwell and James Butterworth	
	Index	136

Citation Information

The chapters in this book were ori   14 (November 2019). When citing this material, please use the original page numbering for each article, as follows:

Introduction
Sivamohan Valluvan and Virinder S. Kalra
Ethnic and Racial Studies, volume 42, issue 14 (November 2019),
pp. 2393–2412

Chapter 1
Deportation, racism and multi-status Britain: immigration control and the production of race in the present
Luke de Noronha
Ethnic and Racial Studies, volume 42, issue 14 (November 2019),
pp. 2413–2430

Chapter 2
More in common: the domestication of misogynist white supremacy and the assassination of Jo Cox
Hannah Jones
Ethnic and Racial Studies, volume 42, issue 14 (November 2019),
pp. 2431–2449

Chapter 3
Conflating the Muslim refugee and the terror suspect: responses to the Syrian refugee "crisis" in Brexit Britain
Madeline-Sophie Abbas
Ethnic and Racial Studies, volume 42, issue 14 (November 2019),
pp. 2450–2469

Chapter 4
Care and cruelty in Chios: the "refugee crisis" and the limits of Europe

Malcolm James
Ethnic and Racial Studies, volume 42, issue 14 (November 2019),
pp. 2470–2489

Chapter 5
Racism and Brexit: notes towards an antiracist populism
Ben Pitcher
Ethnic and Racial Studies, volume 42, issue 14 (November 2019),
pp. 2490–2509

Chapter 6
*"I feel English as fuck": translocality and the performance of alternative
identities through rap*
Richard Bramwell and James Butterworth
Ethnic and Racial Studies, volume 42, issue 14 (November 2019),
pp. 2510–2527

For any permission-related enquiries please visit:
www.tandfonline.com/page/help/permissions

Notes on Contributors

Madeline-Sophie Abbas, Department of Sociology, University of Manchester, UK.

Richard Bramwell, School of Social Sciences, Loughborough University, UK.

James Butterworth, School of Social Sciences, Loughborough University, UK.

Luke de Noronha, Department of Psychosocial Studies, Birkbeck College, University of London, UK; School of Social Science and Public Policy, Keele University, UK.

Malcolm James, School of Media, Film and Music, University of Sussex, UK.

Hannah Jones, Department of Sociology, University of Warwick, UK.

Virinder S. Kalra, Department of Sociology, University of Warwick, UK.

Ben Pitcher, School of Social Sciences, University of Westminster, UK.

Sivamohan Valluvan, Department of Sociology, University of Warwick, UK.

Introduction

Sivamohan Valluvan and Virinder S. Kalra

ABSTRACT

This Introduction first proposes a definitional map applicable to the racial nationalisms currently ascendant in Britain (and Western Europe, more broadly). The paper then outlines the respective contributions to the Special Issue – with an emphasis on the politics of bordering that organizes today so much of nationalism's claim on the state. The second half thereupon establishes a wider conjunctural context within which such analyses can be most productively read. Drawing on Stuart Hall's formative analysis, we argue that it is an understanding of the distinctly *contradictory* drives intrinsic to recent capitalism that is required. Through mapping the uneasy nation/market bind constitutive of the "Little Englander" political subjectivity that Thatcherism forged, this section focuses on the "disjuncture" that has emerged in the intervening period: a disjuncture, compounded by complementary forms of "postcolonial melancholia", that has seen the various nationalist drives in the body politic obtain today a more pronounced political autonomy.

Introduction

Uncertainty continues to prevail since the decision by the British electorate to change the United Kingdom's relationship to Europe. Of course, so very much has been said about "Brexit" that it remains a thankless task to confidently isolate any key prevailing impressions. The nigh unprecedented turn to an inward nationalism – anxious, defensive and resentful – can certainly be attributed to a range of prevailing circumstances. For instance, much analysis has foregrounded the era-defining economic restructuring – as recession, austerity and marketization – by which the twentieth-century social mobility contract has ground to a juddering halt. A contiguous commentary has focused on the increased melancholic revanchism that arises when Europe has ceased to enjoy the global economic privileges and pre-eminence that it has erstwhile been accustomed to (Mbembe 2018a, 1). Even more prominent has been the often apologist claims that the nationalist turn is a "backlash" by silent majorities against the perceived advance of socially liberal norms and demographic reconstitution. Elsewhere, a more generative commentary has foregrounded the destabilizing effects of shifts in our media culture – digital and online affordances that result in a technologically mediated collapse in the legitimacy of elites and state institutions. These mooted themes, in traversing economics, cultural backlash and media structures, preclude in turn a well-harmonized analysis vis-à-vis the resurgence of nationalism.[1]

There does however seem to be one emergent consensus that has taken shape across these disparate accounts: namely, it is increasingly clear that whatever the underlying factors, the European Union (EU) referendum was primarily framed in the popular imagination by the overdetermined issue of immigration and wider cognate anxieties regarding race and ethnic difference.[2] Most overtly, this included the toxic fault-line that EU free movement came to represent in the public debate: both as an internal expanse where Eastern and Southern Europeans are alleged to be enjoying excessive access to Britain's economic and social goods, but also as a conduit for dark-skinned refugees to march across uninhibited to the sweet fields of England. And though less decisive to the public discourse, other similarly charged themes that gained prominence as the referendum campaigning intensified included: the disingenuous hectoring about the prospect of Turkey (read Muslims) acceding to the EU, various coded remarks about the Roma (but also Romanians, who were often publically read through the "Roma frame" [Fox, Moraşanu, and Szilassy 2012]), and even the many strained if ill-informed comments about the tyranny of anti-racist political correctness that ECHR[3] technocrats were said to be upholding (Chowdhury and Shiner, forthcoming). Seen accordingly in its entirety, Brexit signaled one significant instantiation of a successful new nationalist political programme that hinges substantially on the ostensible problems of immigration, multiculturalism, and ethnic diversity more broadly. Indeed, whilst this new nationalist orientation is not without alternatives – as evidenced by some of the resurgent autonomous left organizing that has underpinned the more progressive aspects of Labour's rehabilitation of a social democracy-cum-urban liberalism pivot – it remains a truism to note that the idea of nation has emphatically recovered its political confidence.

But what specifically renders this recourse to nation, nationalism? Whilst cognizant of definitional work's multiple hazards, we tentatively note that today's nationalism might be best understood as the set of discourses by which primary culpability for significant sociopolitical problems, whether real or imagined, is attributed to various ethno-racial communities who are understood as not belonging (Valluvan 2019, 36). Any such definition will seem counter-intuitive when read against the more established literature on the subject. After all, the nation itself can certainly be understood as so much more, relating to various fundamental conceptions (even if misplaced in our opinion) of community, collective culture, historical time, and also wider demarcations of what political sovereignty amounts to in modernity. We do not deny this. Western national*ism* however, as a specific political temperament, trades on a simpler principle – a principle that turns, in the first instance, on the exclusionary politics of Othering.

It might admittedly seem too obvious, too tautological, to say here that the nation is committed to a series of exclusionary distinctions. For instance, the notion of an exclusionary reality is readily apparent in the nation-state imagination's own very proud assertion of its "irremediable particularity" (Anderson, [1983] 2006, 5). This is, in other words, an assertion that is intrinsically exclusionary: put simply, to be something *particular* is to preclude the possibility of being something else. Similarly, the nation-state remains necessarily exclusionary in its very mechanical configuration: the provisioning of passports, voting privileges, welfare rights and so forth does of course exclude those not of that nation-state. (For instance, if one is going to one university, it is likely the case that one is not of a different university; the same prosaic observation might be said of the nation-state.) In turn, in this precise sense of the nation-state's very configuration and claim to being, it might seem all too circular to assert a definitional emphasis on exclusion.

Our contention is however less concerned with the nation in itself. It is instead the specifics of national*ism*, as a distinct political mentality, that is our priority here. Nationalism, to our mind, exceeds a simple descriptive characterization of the nation-state's territorialized institutionalization. Namely, the distinctiveness of contemporary nationalism as a political logic is that it marks a process through which a self-appointed normative majority attributes its putative socioeconomic, cultural and security concerns to the excessive presence and allowance made to those understood as outsiders. Nationalism concerns, in other words, those moments where political discourse reserves an outsized place for the problems putatively posed by those who do not belong. It is herein less an affirmative politics of strong belonging and more a negational politics of aversion and disavowal (Gilroy, [1987] 2002, 49–50; Hall 1992, 188; Yuval-Davis 2006, 204). Needless to say, those who comprise the relevant field of Othered non-belonging include the variously racialized ethnic minorities but also select foreign peoples and/or international forces, some of which intertwine with and reinforce the pathologies attributed to those internal, generally non-white groups (Brubaker 2017).[4]

The anxieties attributed today to such iconic figures of non-belonging assume many guises. These are, for instance, the myriad and at times contradictory anxieties written upon the figure of the migrant – as labour migrant, as welfare tourist, as culturally adversarial refugee, and, albeit less frequently, as crass foreign capitalists. Such assorted anxieties are not however operating in a discursive vacuum neatly contained to figure of the imminent migrant arrival. Instead, the hostility that meets the migrant lies, in part, in its palimpsest quality – where the pathologization of immigration is written upon the well-rehearsed scripts by which the nation's already existing internal Others have been characterized (Gilroy, [1987] 2002). As far as Britain is concerned, these include the anxieties attributed to the black city and its criminal propensities and, of course, the increasingly trenchant anxieties tied to the Muslim – as culturally regressive, misogynist, violent, proselytizing, and, perhaps most invidiously, as fecund, protean and ungrateful (Hage 2017).

It is uncontroversial to note that the electoral map is being emphatically remade by the advances of these above political assertions, assertions that demand less equivocating responses to the threats these multiple but often overlapping outsiders represent. Relatedly, nationalist solutions increasingly obtain a panacean value in the popular imagination, suggesting that various challenges characteristic of the present will dissipate through both reducing the presence of such significant Others as well as formally circumscribing their scope for disruption. And importantly, these anxieties that cluster around such a multiplying cast of nationalist disavowal also convert into forceful political demands upon the state. It is namely via specific state contexts that these fears manifest, organize and propagate – wherein public institutions become the site at which these fears become a repressive reality. Put differently, such nationalist assertions are not only discursive "distortions" of the political but they are also active claims upon state practice. Indeed, as put in the memorable words of Arendt ([1951] 1973, 275), nationalism might be best seen as the terms by which the "the nation conquers the state".

Today's bending of the British state towards more avowedly nationalist imperatives is increasingly undeniable. Consider here, alongside the summary end to EU free movement that Brexit most starkly represents, the much discussed "hostile environment" and its policy aim to make immanent the "illegalization" (de Genova 2002) of denizens deemed expendable/undesirable. Consider too the wider attempts to further render welfare access contingent to immigration status, the stripping of student visas of the right to work, the entrenchment of prohibitive salary thresholds as regards work-permits, as well as the gutting of family reunification protections. Parallel to this move to "erect the barricades" (Malik 2018) vis-à-vis immigration, which remains the archetypically populist instruction of our era, we also see in Britain a complementary recourse to integrationist measures – already rehearsed during Blairism via the turn towards "community cohesion" policies but further entrenched in the notorious Casey Review of 2016 and the wider machinations of contemporary Tory-led governments. This is a resurgent integration conceit (Back et al. 2002; Kundnani 2007; McGhee 2008) that trades on an unequivocally nationalist premise: presuming that the coherence and integrity of the nation, in its distinctly majoritarian sense, is being imperiled by the excess presence of "alien" cultures (not least, Muslims) incompatible with the national polity – alien cultures that are in need of remedial redress and/or active proscription.

A proper social science reckoning with contemporary nationalism requires in turn a conjoined emphasis, one that is able to unpack the prominence of various racialized Others in underpinning the renewed appeal of the nation's political mandate but also tracking how this translates into assorted institutional practices as guided by nationalism. This is not to exhaust the centrality of racialized outsiders to nationalist projects in the West, but it simply reconfirms the importance of race (and as the far as the UK is concerned, imperialism) to any credible account of that very project.

Bordering, exclusion and nationalist statecraft

This Special Issue will accordingly navigate today's reconsolidated nationalism by addressing its affinity to multiple racialized narratives and attendant state practices. Unsurprisingly, a recurring emphasis of many of the articles centres on the dehumanization of the refugee and therein the constitutive fortification and violences that flow from this dehumanization. This emphasis is a deliberate one, ably attending to a theme that has become the centrepiece of much contemporary analysis of racial nationalisms: i.e. the border and bordering. Whilst much early twenty-first-century writing in Europe situated the toxic racial politics of nation within the policy mantras of integration/community cohesion agendas, there has been a concerted turn in recent research towards the hard materiality of borders (Anderson 2013; El-Enany 2019; Yuval-Davis, Wemyss, and Cassidy 2018). Luke de Noronha's contribution to this Special Issue acts in turn as a particularly generative distillation of this emergent writing on the border – noting how it is through border practices that race-meaning often gets made and assigned, leading to the codified stratification of human worth and disposability as well as rendering those who obtain less-than-citizen status vulnerable to different forms of economic exploitation (Bhattacharyya 2018). Building implicitly upon Back et al.'s (2018, 138) reading of how fragmented citizenship status and practices of migrant vilification intersect to constitute "new hierarchies of belonging", de Noronha brings into sharp relief the centrality of border practices to today's social and political constitution. He also gives unique attention to how the "race-making" done through bordering has found particularly sharp expression through the multiplying deportation regimes common to modern statecraft. Distinctive about de Noronha's contribution here is the attentiveness to the intimately told human tragedies that accrue through the otherwise impersonal materiality of border-practice. Drawing upon a rich vein of ethnographic writing, de Noronha allows the narratives of two black men (Jason and Ricardo) deported to Jamaica to take centre-stage, finding in their pained recollections of a life denied the unique mechanisms by which bordering and racialization intertwine – a logic that, in the instances of Jason and Ricardo, reaches for racialized conceptions of criminality and expendability in refusing people the only place they've known, since childhood, to be home (London).

The violence of bordering that de Noronha foregrounds is not however to be situated only at the level of the state. As has been widely commented upon with heightened alarm, the racialized logics demanding the consolidation of the nation (Jones et al. 2017) does also sublimate into a pointed form of civic violence. Put differently, the increasingly militant assertions of national ruination that a treacherously "liberal" ruling class is said to be presiding over gradually emboldens an appetite for vigilante fascism. As Hannah Jones argues in this Special Issue, the murder of the pro-Remain MP Jo Cox by a far-right sympathizer was a particularly stark moment that signals the intensified violence that this nationalist threshold threatens. Jones accordingly employs a highly textured reading of how the lethal violence exercised by members of the public is not only sourced in existing dominant discursive frameworks, but equally, the violence itself becomes denied, reframed and/or seen as exceptional aberrations, not warranting any meaningful political reflection.[5] In other words, this case also illustrates the way in which the security state works through racialized conceptions of who constitutes a threat: i.e. the "Muslim male" as a distinctly "cultural" problem versus Jo Cox's murderer as the proverbial "lone wolf" with a history of mental health troubles.

However, as opposed to it being merely an indication of racial nationalism's incendiary horizons, Jones also focuses on the grassroots resistance that finds expression in the wake of such moments. It is evident that such threshold moments can act as a galvanizing node around which a popular dissent can congeal; but, as Jones again notes, the possibilities of popular resistance that emerged in the aftermath of the murder of Jo Cox are not without their own contradictions. Jones demonstrates how the resistance that might be construed as "mainstream" often tends towards highly patriarchal renditions of opposition circumscribed by liberal propriety – yielding, in turn, ineffectual and at times complicit forms of resistance. For instance, as Jones asks, is it sufficient or even practicable to simply assert a populist rhetoric of commonality against a perceived politics of "hate" and "division"? Does the more politically durable move lie instead in a more confrontational politics, nurturing much more avowedly radical alternatives regarding the conceptions of belonging and primordial origins that are otherwise the preserve of the nation-myth that the far right deploys so effectively?

Madeline-Sophie Abbas's article explores a similar tension in how the popular challenge to anti-refugee politics often calls upon a language of liberal humanism and yet it is that self-same language which subsequently becomes prominent in discrediting the desirability of refugees – e.g. prospective refugees as the bearers of illiberal cultures and pathology. Abbas develops here an arresting notion of the "concentrationary gothic"; a concept which helps explore how the barbarisms as ascribed to the spectre of the Muslim – scripts that reach deep into the colonial archive of Orientalist "demonology" (Said, [1978] 2003, 26) – stunt and undo any initial compulsion towards "compassion". Malcolm James's paper extends and situates these contradictions within the more visceral frontline that the Mediterranean today represents. The so-called "refugee crisis", more properly understood as the human crisis produced by state-enforced borders (Trilling 2019), has become perhaps the starkest expression of contemporary nationalism's human detritus. A callous matrix of cruelty has been erected across the Mediterranean – wherein camps, border patrols, traffickers, and vigilante nativist mobs at sea and on land, all interweave to realize a thick web of dehumanization geared towards repelling the refugees fleeing war, environmental degradation and/or abject poverty. These are namely the multiple mechanisms constitutive of a "Fortress Europe" that render real the "death-worlds" (Mbembe 2003) in which people are left to die and/or endure a perpetual wretchedness. James, drawing poetically upon his own experience volunteering at one of the epicentres of this human crisis (the Greek island of Chios), patiently tracks the projections of this cruelty. James does not however leave the reader only with this dense miasma of cruelty, insisting upon the alternative structures of care that also emerged in the midst of the crisis – improvised circuits of care that tie together refugees' resourceful efforts to assist each other, local residents' makeshift attempts to provision everyday support and solidarity, as well as the concerned volunteers from across the world that descended upon these frontline Greek locations. It is accordingly these interweaving webs of "care and cruelty" that James places at the heart of the reconsolidated racial nationalisms that the European continent is once again contending with. James warns against only seeing in the present an unassailable sea of cruelty, implicitly arguing that to render cruelty the sole object of analysis is to render it sublime – a sublimity that invites, in time, a resigned quietism.

These respective articles help us think herein about how a confident antinationalist politics would first have to mobilize against the distinct racial work the national border currently does. It is at the border where the most rabid racial formulations of a nationalist politics are most emphatically invested; and it is accordingly at the border that such politics can be most meaningfully challenged. Such interventions become particularly salutary when recognizing that the concerted anti-immigrant and neo-imperial[6] politics of borders is hardly a unique preserve of the right, whether extreme or mainstream (Mondon and Winter 2017). It is apparent that many on the left too have become reattached to the border as a political horizon, whereby, through conviction and/or opportunism, they see in politics of immigration and community a possibility for populist appeal. This renewed left nationalism was endorsed in particularly slapdash terms in Nagle's (2018) now well-flogged "The Left Case for Borders" as well as in the proliferation across Europe of "new" left parties that press anti-immigration positions.[7] But it is also apparent in the frustrating indecision of the current Labour leadership who, though issuing some not insubstantial critiques of detention and deportation, still seem resolutely wedded to a reassertion of border control as well as frequently rehabilitating those nationalist mantras that work through a white working-class mythology.

Indeed, a particularly awkward fact about the current political repertoire is that a newly confident nationalist politics is able to present itself as the voice of the dispossessed, the working class, the welfare state, and other cognate left-of-centre twentieth century emphases. This is a form of nationalist positioning that presses a pronounced sense of class injury and various putatively "anti-establishment" allusions. There is, of course, a perennially frustrating disconnect here – where the nationalist claim to anti-market and/or anti-establishment solidarity is contradicted by its more immediate harangues against other marginalized working-class communities (existing minorities) and outsiders (migrants and refugees), rendering their presence undesirable whilst also undercutting any even residual notion of a decidedly global anti-capitalist identification. It is against this context that Ben Pitcher sets out in this Special Issue a series of original inquiries. Does a sustained challenge against nationalist discourses also have to consequently interrogate it as a matter of "form"; wherein, it becomes necessary to ask how contemporary nationalism has become contoured by an anti-establishment populism and what kind of complication does this pose to the task of resistance and critique? Put differently, does a straightforward assertion of anti-racism without robustly contesting the anti-establishment paraphernalia that couches populist demagoguery simply lend further credibility to the nationalist conceit? Similarly, as follows the necessarily introspective turn in contemporary left theory (Fassin 2019; Mouffe 2018), Pitcher sensitively asks whether the anti-racist left requires its own competing populist discourse or is populism, by the very nature of its underlying premises, the preserve of normative nativism?

Pitcher helps in turn press this Special Issue towards the contradictory tensions that suffuse both the assertions of but also challenges to nationalism's heightened appeal. It is also here that this Special Issue's final article profiles a series of generative questions. Richard Bramwell and James Butterworth's contribution reminds us, in contrast to the nativist circumscribing of what national belonging entails, that research needs to stay alive to the many intuitively cosmopolitan renditions of belonging that also vie for prominence. The authors give extended attention here to how young urban minorities, through the *practices* that underpin popular cultural expression such as grime and hip-hop, ably claim the nation in an unapologetic and irreverent manner. Developing an original sense of the "translocality" that suffuses black-led urban cultural expression, Bramwell and Butterworth foreground how an alternative conception of English belonging becomes rooted across those cities characterized by multiculture. They consequently ask whether this rhizomatic cultural geography that stitches together cities as scattered across England can represent a productive counterpoint to how the nation might be popularly engaged; this being an engagement that is thoroughly indifferent to the "pastoral" visioning of English idylls and white homogeneity and sets instead a decidedly diverse and decidedly disheveled aesthetic of the city as the focal point of belonging.

These questions that Bramwell and Butterworth revive are certainly not new. The decorated tradition of British Cultural Studies that they build upon has consistently flagged the political promise of those urban cultures as developed in the crucible of diasporic culture hostile to the illusory clarity and comforts of communitarian belonging. Put differently, the multiethnic urban margins have often acted as the vanguard for alternative templates of an "unkempt and unruly" (Gilroy 2004, x) multicultural belonging. The reach of such politics is however frequently frustrated by various structural demarcations – contending with state criminalization of the cultural practices associated with blackness; the inevitable limits of "youth" cultural orientations and subcultural isolation; as well as the wider forms of commercialized cooption that might defuse the otherwise subversive strain intrinsic to such cultural expression. These are questions that left cultural theory has always had to contend with and they remain tensions that Bramwell and Butterworth write through with a considered balance: wherein, to insist upon alternative horizons, as sourced in the minor keys of today, always remains, however thankless, a fundamental task for critical analysis that is also affirmative.

Capitalism, "authoritarian populism" and "Little Englander" nationalisms

In sum, the above papers all profile a nationalist crisis where the refugee and the migrant become the primary objects of political discourse and the border the primary political solution. It is, however, the case that today's nationalist positioning, and the racial demons that such positioning turns on, is often subjected to a materialist analysis – one which reads such politics as symptomatic of wider economic stagnation, "austerity doctrine", and post-industrial abjections more broadly. Whilst this is certainly important, it is also apparent that such epiphenomenal readings often tend towards a flattened reductionism that not only circumvents an analytic feel for contradiction but also disregards the specific question of why precisely does the nation and whiteness become such inviting conduits through which people are meant to make sense of the economic distress they experience. Put bluntly, the outstanding question that remains unanswered here is why is the political solution to capitalist crisis to be found so affirmatively in enhanced state powers vis-à-vis border control.

The place of capitalist developments in calibrating and/or galvanizing nationalism does remain important to any meaningful analysis. Indeed, in seeking to formulate a response to the crises instantiated by the demand for withdrawal from the EU, we convened in 2016 a workshop at the University of Manchester. Our immediate aim was to collect the insights provided by Stuart Hall in his formative analysis of "authoritarian populism" and its pivotal place in the broader politics of what he famously coined as "Thatcherism". The papers in this Special Issue derive from that workshop, but do perhaps, in retrospect, owe more to themes of "moral panic" and "folk devils" as foregrounded in *Policing the Crisis*, another enduring text by Hall et al. ([1978] 2013) and colleagues. We take the liberty, therefore, of reasserting in the remainder of this Introduction the necessity of thinking more directly through capitalism's relationship to the wider politics of nation, race and the migrant outsider. Doing so establishes a wider context within which to situate the respective contributors' engagement of today's racial nationalisms.

Interrogating the relationship between the nationalism and capitalism (Davidson 2017) is no simple exercise. Our intention therefore is only to sketch, employing a Hallsian temperament, the importance of economic restructuring and class re-composition in accounting for contemporary politics whilst simultaneously refusing to allow such economic readings to take on a misplaced causal pre-eminence nor allowing such economic formulations to be read independently of cultural formations.

As has been widely observed, today's nationalism presses multiple motifs that appeal to a sense of (white) working class and small town dignity that is increasingly presented as imperiled. Such appeals operate quite obviously outside of and/or against a neoliberal premise (Virdee and McGeever 2018); but, crucially, this is also a nationalism that flows out of the very Thatcherite political pivot that consolidated that self-same neoliberal premise. It is worth remembering that the popular thrust of Thatcherism hinged on a pointed mythologization of aspirational working-class uplift as well as an entrepreneurial petit-bourgeois provincialism (best understood through the iconography of the shopkeeper that Thatcher, through her own biography, ably embodied). We see however that this sociocultural compact that authorized her parallel politics of zealous privatization has obtained today a more pronounced political autonomy. This is an autonomy borne out of marketization's more formal material failures but also because such marketization has become incrementally ensconced within a wider mythology of global supranational politics (including the EU) that often contradicts with the imagery of provincial thrift that Thatcher took care to foreground so steadfastly.

In prizing open this densely knotted contradiction, it is Hall's (2018) writing on the crisis of the 1970s and 1980s that is formative here. Whilst it would be theoretically slapdash to suggest that there are multiple Capitalisms, it can be less controversially mooted that there are always multiple capitalist "rationalities" (Brown 2006, 690) – insofar as, there are multiple often competing cultural formations constitutive of the body politic into which capitalism, as respective to its conjunctural exigencies, nestles itself. Hall's prescient remarks in 1979 about the emergent cultural conceits that he surveyed on the eve of Thatcher's first electoral triumph reveal particularly well how any such capitalist leap makes an active but always uncertain claim on the textures of the popular. As he said at the time, "There is still some debate as to whether [Thatcherism] is likely to be short-lived or long-term, a movement of the surface or something more deeply lodged in the body politic" (Hall 1979, 14).

The cultural discourse Hall was bringing into view was one where the "vigorous virtues" as ascribed to the industrious petit-bourgeois shopkeeper ("energetic", "self-reliant", anti-taxation) was firmly situated within a wider mythopoeia of the English character – as rustic, suburban, homely, respectable, familial and defensively "robust" (Evans and Taylor 1996, 226). Equally, in asserting this distinct cultural modelling of the national subject *qua* provincial entrepreneur, a series of "folk devils" were identified (Hall et al. [1978] 2013): a series of dangerous portends and iconic sources of disruption against whom a respectable provincial Englishness (and the wider mandate of a "sadist state" [Brown 1988, 3]) was asserted. Key figures that took such enduring shape here was of course the black "mugger" of the inner city; the culturally adversarial immigrant "swamping" the realm; and, also, a legion of allegedly deracinated leftist ideologues – both "metropolitan cultural elites" and pugnacious trade union subversives alike – who offend the English calling and mentality.

Much of this might be already well documented (Featherstone 2017; James and Valluvan 2018), but it is worth reiterating, lest Thatcherism risk being misunderstood as an abstracted exultation of "homo economicus", lacking in any broader cultural figuration. And crucially, whilst the mobilizing of a particular commonsense – impressionistically sketched here as a Little Englander entrepreneurialism – can certainly licence capitalist work (neoliberal marketization), it is also the case that such "commonsenses" often sit uneasily vis-à-vis the broader capitalist project they have been harnessed to. As once noted by the idiosyncratic Gray (2010, 19) regarding the always-apparent contradictions between the dreamscapes and market principles respectively constitutive of Thatcherism:

> [Thatcher] fully shared Hayek's view that free markets reinforce "traditional values", which is an inversion of their actual effect. The conservative country of which she dreamed had more in common with Britain in the 1950s, an arte-fact of Labour collectivism, than it did with the one that emerged from her free-market policies. [For instance], a highly mobile labour market enforces a regime of continuous change. The type of personality that thrives in these conditions is the opposite of the stolid, dutiful bourgeois Thatcher envisioned.

Gray's observation, though operating in a very different context to ours, helps clarify that any such cultural modelling – and its assorted cognitive sensibil-ities, symbolic affinities, and affective investments – is conjunctural, and is fre-quently jolted when the broader capitalist contract it is wedded to is itself restructured. In short, what requires acknowledgement here is that whilst appeals to nation can indeed do the bidding of broader capitalist exigencies, the appeal of nation, once re-galvanized, often exceeds, contradicts and/or subverts that initial capitalist programme.

These reflections allow in turn for a more effective transposing of Hall's seminal sense of *conjuncture* to the present's distinctive sense of *disjuncture*. Prevailing sociological analysis often misses the fact that today's nationalism is not simply a diversionary attempt to fill the political void that a capitalist crisis engenders. It is instead a fetid amplification of the nationalism that was already so deeply threaded through the capitalist restructuring as "sutured" (Hall 1996, 3) in the late 1970s/early 1980s (James 2018). Put simply, the present reveals only a marked deformation of this already fragile nation/capital alliance. When a faith in capitalist social mobility dissi-pates so resolutely, what remains of that residual governmental culture is only the rump of provincial nationalism that had dutifully complemented that initial faith in capitalist evangelism but was never simply secondary to it (Toscano 2017).

This is accordingly a provincial nationalism that has today been made starkly visible on its own terms, intensifying in confidence amid its partial dis-lodging from the broader capitalist thesis. Put differently, this newly liberated nationalism can still do the bidding of capitalist mantras, but it can also be rallied as a populist critique of capitalism – as anti-establishment, as anti-elite, as anti-globalization, and as nominally pro-welfare. This is, however, a cri-tique of capitalism that, in the final instance, necessarily favours nationalist nostrums. It is, in other words, a vernacular critique that attributes to the hordes of migrants and inauthentic insider minorities a variety of pathologies vis-à-vis economic duress – as work-shy, as exploiting welfare state largesse, as further crowding an already distressed labour market, as straining resources, and as impinging upon scarce public and residential space.

Relatedly, it also rails against the alleged generosity of development aid and/ or against the unfair financial advantages that foreign entities are said to obtain at Britain's expense, not least through EU contributions. In sum, this is a redirected anti-neoliberalism that only admits the nation (and is constitutive appeals and demons) as the valid site of political intervention and redress.

This partial unmooring of nationalism from neoliberal imperatives remains to us an analytic angle that is all too often neglected in contemporary accounts of Brexit and cognate themes. But whilst such an attunement to the disjuncture of nationalism to neoliberal capitalism is important, equally relevant are the contrasting terms by which neoliberalism itself can become consumed by nationalism. Emergent analysis has begun to draw some attention to how the Brexit sponsored nationalisms currently prevalent cut across a decidedly contradictory relationship to capitalism. A contradiction that might be provisionally typified as the aforementioned petit-bourgeois protectionism that foregrounds a politics of provincial insularity, and on the other hand, a corporate multinational capitalism (global neoliberalism) still ostensibly committed to its ideal of borderless trade and access. However, what also remains important for us here is a different dimension – one where neoliberalism exists not only as a principle of global market dynamism but can also wield its own distinct brand of bordered nativism.

It is, of course, clear today that neoliberal capitalism does hew towards a sustained lobbying for the EU. This is however only one expression of neoliberalism's political vocabulary. There is also another neoliberal rationale that is not straightforwardly anti-nationalism, and, indeed, calls for its own brand of nationalist consolidation. Contrary to the often-Marxist readings of neoliberalism as summarily hostile to the nation, neoliberalism does in fact routinely press a very marked attachment to the politics of bordering and its attendant anti-immigration harangues. This is namely a programme that desires a streamlining of the border and the "human capital" considerations (Davies 2017) against which immigration is to be appraised. Made most explicit in Ian Duncan Smith's candid remarks that "we [have] had a huge number of very low-value ... people coming through the EU" (Brinkhurst-Cuff 2017), neoliberalism does in fact wish to assume very clinical ownership over the border – a border that is made to the measure of the exploitable labour that capital most desires at any select moment. This neoliberal foundation that conceives of the nation as enterprise (Davies 2014; Mirowski and Plehwe 2009) – and its population, therein, as a pooling of skill-sets and capitals – ably hitches itself to wider racial regimes by which people are deemed worthwhile, capable, and enterprising. A neoliberal remit does accordingly often court the politics of nation and its constitutive border instruments (e.g. immigration controls, fixed-term work visas, salary-thresholds, work restrictions on student visas, and the hollowing out of family unification protections). To intuitively assume that the neoliberal and the nationalist are mutually adversarial remains herein a misnomer, and a dangerous one at that.

Indeed, as follows an oft-neglected analysis of Hardt and Negri, the migrant might even be read as a figure who *refuses* the capitalist order. This might seem counterintuitive, but it is in the very act of rejecting the capitalist designation of a geographically stratified class role that the migrant becomes a disruptive, even cataclysmic, body. As they put it in their defining *Empire*, "Mobility and mass worker nomadism [...] always expresses a refusal and a search for liberation: the resistance against the horrible conditions of exploitation and the search for freedom and new conditions of life" (Hardt and Negri 2000, 212). Put differently, whilst migrants might at times act as the reserve army of labour or a substratum of the proletariat (Miles 1982) open to heightened forms of exploitation, the migrant does also render volatile the ethnonational territorialization that global capitalism solicits. That neoliberalism, as a governmental logic, might become re-enchanted by the border and its specific mandates is not herein entirely surprising when contextualized within this broader structural relationship of migration and "fixity" to capitalism (Mbembe 2018b). Capitalism has, in other words, always pressed a fixity/fluidity simultaneity – where enhanced mobility for some acts in concert with the attempted immobilizing/thwarting of others (Bhattacharyya 2018). It is, accordingly, this split that helps further contextualize today's neoliberal fascination with nationalist assertion – an assertion that even threatens at times to override the underlying capitalist thesis.

Conclusion

That the Thatcherism documented in Hall's formative analysis would culminate in the neoliberal "supernova" (Duman et al. 2018) of Cameron's austerity and marketization blitz was not unexpected. But that the same Thatcherism would culminate, through a different genealogy, in the nationalism of today is also not unexpected. We have asked accordingly that the sociology of nationalism and capitalism alike must stay more alive to how what was once a conjunctural affinity becomes, in time, the disjuncture of tomorrow. Affinities of capital and nation often come undone, gaining new autonomies and making political demands that are not always initially evident when first drafted.

This reading of a capitalist conjuncture's contingencies has tried in turn to draw upon Hall's formative reading of capital and culture as perennially entangling and disentangling. One catalysing cultural logic that was however relatively muted in Hall's analysis is what Gilroy (2004) has named more recently as the distortions that arise via a wider longing for imperial time – a "melancholia" that has taken on a more turbulent charge in the intervening political period. There is, in other words, a more psychoanalytic dimension that obtains when explicating any such nationalist rationality as articulated in its distinctly British mode. There is, after all, a thoroughly awkward embrace of past imperial hymns that renders Britain's political logics vis-à-vis the nation and sovereignty sufficiently unique in form (Ashe 2016; El-Enany 2018). Put differently, and borrowing opportunistically from Gramsci's ([1930] 2011, 33) memorable phrasing, it is possible to distil here those distinctly "morbid symptoms" that arise in the "interregnum" period that characterizes Britain's contemporary political culture: a period bookended by a remembered imperial supremacy on the one hand, and, on the other, a future order, exacerbated by climate breakdown perhaps, where British capitalism is reconciled to a more humble self-narration befitting of its "provincial" place in the world.

There is, for instance, a recurring threat by arch-Brexiters to oversee a bonfire of any existing regulatory and fiscal check on capitalist evangelism – including the evisceration of workers' rights, environmental and consumer regulations, as well as other redistributive and equality encumbrances. Even the much-discussed possibility of defaulting to WTO settings could be construed as a partial expression of this aspiration (Luyendijk 2017). The underlying intimation is that a "Britannia" thus "unchained" (Kwarteng et al. 2012) stands to recover a leading market position in the global economy. This will certainly seem to most foreign observers a comical delusion – a notion of restored British glory in an era, not least, of "Chinese globalization" (Shilliam 2018, 175) being a particularly quixotic proposition. But it is the specific psychoanalysis of this hubris that remains for us politically consequential. What Gilroy (2004) calls melancholia trades on a hazily glimpsed and distinctly prettified sense of the putative moral clarity, public stability and global supremacy that colonial pre-war whiteness invokes – experiencing that past as prematurely lost and precipitating only abject decline and dysfunction. Melancholy is herein bleak and "pathological" (98), prone to sublimating into a brinkmanship commanding political decisions so markedly anachronistic vis-à-vis the present circumstances and possibilities with which the state refuses to reconcile itself. And though this melancholia is usually couched within a broader conservative and/or a vernacular left temperament, it is increasingly evident that such melancholia can also claim for itself a more niche neoliberal register.

However, as Gilroy also helped clarify, the playing out of an imperial delusion and misremembered time of social and moral coherence should not be seen *only* as a parlous political brinkmanship (though much of Brexit is certainly that [O'Toole, 2018]). Whilst any such capitalist sovereignty as presided over by the nation-state of "Rule Britannia" vintage (Dorling and Tomlinson 2019) cannot be resurrected, what this imperial hubris can certainly do is further glory in the revanchist politics of racial Othering that the politics of nation solicits: further anti-immigration harangues; further engage in high-profile demonstrations of bordering (via "Go Home" vans, the deportation of black "criminals", and the "citizenship deprivation" of pariah Muslims

[Kapoor 2019]); further engage in foolhardy neo-imperial wars and/or postures; and further circumscribe welfare-state entitlements along implicit invocations of authentically white working-class "deservingness" (Shilliam 2018; see also Bhambra 2017; Narayan 2017). This "postcolonial melancholia" is herein not one that is oriented only towards implosion; it is also a melancholia that surveys the flesh and blood objects worthy of sharp rebuke (be it the EU and its constitutive migrants, but also, and more enduringly, the various iconic Others already in the nation's midst). The fact that the one abiding "red line" that Brexit proponents of all vintages (including its neoliberal cheerleaders) will not compromise on is the end to "free movement" – construed materially as immigration within the EU but also acting as a proxy expression of anti-immigrant sentiment more broadly – remains for us a particularly illustrative indication of this redirected melancholic populism.

The melancholic adds in turn a unique affective field – operating through the textures of loss, mourning, solace and also hubris – to the broader nationalist energies as released through the conjunctural unwinding that this paper has hinted at. In other words, the second half of this Introduction has attempted to understand how the nationalisms consolidated by the Brexit impasse cut across a decidedly contradictory relationship to capitalism – a contradiction that induces a whole variety of nationalist expressions, be it neoliberal, anti-neoliberal, or post-neoliberal. And, as Virdee and McGeever (2018) intimate, it is this very contradiction – or, properly put, a failure to read this contradiction – that has yielded such floundering analysis amongst a left intelligentsia of what the current political upheaval represents. Unable to read across the competing capitalist projects, so-called "Lexiters"[8] have read the not insignificant working-class Leave vote[9] as well as the multinational and establishment (e.g. CBI) affinity to the EU and free-movement as a signal indication of today's nationalism constituting a valid (even if partly misdirected) anti-capitalist politics. Conversely, those leftists who intuitively oppose nationalism have understandably seen the provincial middle-class backing of Brexit, and Tory support more broadly, as undermining any ascription to it of an anti-capitalist yearning. But such critics have also at times failed to see that petit bourgeois and aspirational working-class investment in the textures and promises of nationalist reconsolidation is not in itself a capitalist politics (as in, furthering the baseline imperatives of accumulation and rent-seeking). We have argued that this is instead best read as a morality and political sensibility sourced in a particular era of capitalism – namely, "Little Englander" Thatcherism – that is now operating, to some significant degree, outside of a neatly contained capitalist drive.

The relevance of this analysis is two-fold. It first gestures at the particular historical context within which the distinctiveness of contemporary nationalism was seeded. Secondly, it frames the explicitly capitalist conditions within which this nationalism was nursed, but it also names the terms by which this

RACIAL NATIONALISMS

nationalism becomes partially dislodged from that initial affinity to capitalism. The concluding intention of any such analysis, though only outlined in rather impressionistic terms as befitting an introductory statement, is to simply guard against certain recurring tendencies of a left analytic temperament. Whilst the worst of bad Marxism still sees the nation as hosting a popular vernacular as well as providing the figurations of collectivity through which anti-capitalist politics can be pursued; the best of prevailing Marxist orthodoxies have a complacent tendency to see nationalism as surfacing only in the interests of crisis resolution, diversion and "false consciousness". Either way, we have used the closing stretch of this Introduction to note that today's nationalism operates with an autonomy and confidence that, whilst possible to situate within capitalism, cannot be made to bend towards either capitalist or anti-capitalist programmes (when seen as coherent and discrete positions). Put bluntly, nation is not available for conversion, left wing or otherwise.

Notes

1. See Leddy-Owen (2019) and Norris and Inglehart (2019) for overviews of these causal theses currently prevalent.
2. See Gupta and Virdee (2018) for a crisp account of this centrality of race to today's nationalisms.
3. In populist discussion of the EU, the much-maligned European Convention on Human Rights (ECHR) is mistakenly conflated with the EU, when in fact the ECHR predates the formalisation of EU authority and will remain active even upon any possible EU exit – unless formally annulled in a separate capacity.
4. For instance, the febrile escalation of anti-EU campaigning in the run-up to the referendum drew pointed attention to how the refugees gathering across Europe threatened to replenish the already excessive minority groups within the UK – with whom the hordes at the gates share a ostensible commonality, via Islam, skin colour, or country of origin. This was made most notoriously visible in the "Breaking Point" posted fronted by Nigel Farage.
5. Clover (2017) recently captured this tendency towards willful ahistoricism with an easy aphoristic elegance: as he put it, in the media sphere of hot-take shock at every far-right gain or action, "the world begins anew each day".
6. Insofar as, the contemporary practices of deportation and deprivation are concerned.
7. See here the Sahra Wagenknecht-led "Aufstehen" initiative in Germany as well as the positions taken of late by France's Jean-Luc Mélenchon (Adler 2019). But of particularly ominous relevance here is the recent electoral victory in Denmark of Mette Frederiksen's Social Democrats; Frederiksen has overseen an aggressive acquiescence of the Social Democrats to the principles of hard-bordering and integrationist militancy as previously pressed by the populist Danish People's Party (Henley 2019).
8. See two recent interviews with Gilroy where he contends that the "Lexiter" position is a "replaying" (Gilroy et al. 2019, 183) of the Bennite tendency ("the Benn school of English socialism") of yesteryear, a tendency that, "whatever [its] other qualities", constituted a key target for Gilroy (2019) in his landmark *There Aint No*

Black in the Union Jack: "I wanted people to identify and enter the uncomfortable space where Bennism and Powellism could be shown to be adjacent."

9. The precise class composition of the referendum vote, despite the simplifications of tabloid punditry, remains hotly contested. For an instructive reading, see Dorling, Stuart, and Stubbs (2016) and Sayer (2017).

Disclosure statement

No potential conflict of interest was reported by the authors.

References

Adler, D. 2019. "Meet Europe's Left Nationalists." *Nation*, January 10. https://www.thenation.com/article/meet-europes-left-nationalists/.

Anderson, B. [1983] 2006. *Imagined Communities: Reflections on the Origins and Spread of Nationalism*. London: Verso.

Anderson, B. 2013. *Us & Them? The Dangerous Politics of Immigration Control*. Oxford: Oxford University Press.

Arendt, H. [1951] 1973. *The Origins of Totalitarianism*. London: Harvest Books.

Ashe, S. 2016. "UKIP, Brexit and Postcolonial Melancholy." *Discover Society*, 33, June 1. https://discoversociety.org/2016/06/01/ukip-brexit-and-postcolonial-melancholy/.

Back, L., S. Sinha, C. Bryan, V. Baraku, and M. Yemba. 2018. *Migrant City*. London: Routledge.

Back, L., M. Keith, A. Khan, K. Shukra, and J. Solomos. 2002. "New Labour's White Heart: Politics, Multiculturalism and the Return of Assimilation." *The Political Quarterly* 73 (4): 445–454.

Bhambra, G. 2017. "Brexit, Trump, and "Methodological Whiteness": On the Misrecognition of Race and Class." *The British Journal of Sociology* 68 (1): S214–S232.

Bhattacharyya, G. 2018. *Rethinking Racial Capitalism: Questions of Reproduction and Survival*. London: Rowman and Littlefield.

Brinkhurst-Cuff, C. 2017. "Meeting Britain's 'Low-Value Immigrants'." *Vice*, May 28. https://www.vice.com/en_uk/article/bjg494/meeting-britains-low-value-immigrants.

Brown, G. 1988. "Thatcherism." *London Review of Books* 11 (3): 3–4.

Brown, W. 2006. "American Nightmare: Neoliberalism, Neoconservatism, and de-Democratization." *Political Theory* 34 (6): 690–714.

Brubaker, R. 2017. "Between Nationalism and Civilizationism: The European Populist Moment in Comparative Perspective." *Ethnic and Racial Studies* 40 (8): 1191–1226.

Chowdhury, T., and B. Shiner. forthcoming. "The Human Rights Act, Neoliberalism and Populism."

Clover, J. 2017. "Free Speech Year." *Los Angeles Review of Books: Blog*, September 21. https://blog.lareviewofbooks.org/essays/free-speech-year/.

Davidson, N. 2017. "The National Question, Class and the European Union: An Interview with Neil Davidson." *Salvage*, July 22. http://salvage.zone/online-exclusive/the-national-question-class-and-the-european-union-neil-davidson/.

Davies, W. 2014. *The Limits of Neoliberalism: Authority, Sovereignty and the Logic of Competition*. London: Sage.

Davies, W. 2017. "What is "Neo" about Neoliberalism?" *New Republic*, July 13. https://newrepublic.com/article/143849/neo-neoliberalism.

de Genova, N. 2002. "Migrant 'Illegality' and Deportability in Everyday Life." *Annual Review of Anthropology* 31: 419–447.

Dorling, D., B. Stuart, and J. Stubbs. 2016. "Brexit, Inequality and the Demographic Divide." *LSE Blogs: British Politics and Policy*, December 22. https://blogs.lse.ac.uk/politicsandpolicy/brexit-inequality-and-the-demographic-divide/.

Dorling, D., and S. Tomlinson. 2019. *Rule Britannia: Brexit and the End of Empire*. London: Biteback Publishing.

Duman, A., D. Hancox, M. James, and A. Minton. 2018. *Regeneration Songs: Sounds of Investment and Loss in East London*. London: Repeater.

El-Enany, N. 2018. "The Next British Empire." *IPPR Progressive Review* 25 (1): 30–38.

El-Enany, N. 2019. *(B)Ordering Britain: Law, Race and Empire*. Manchester: Manchester University Press.

Evans, B., and A. Taylor. 1996. *Salisbury and Major: Continuity and Change in Conservative Politics*. Manchester: Manchester University Press.

Fassin, E. 2019. *Populism Left and Right*. Chicago, IL: Prickly Paradigm Press.

Featherstone, D. 2017. "Stuart Hall and our Current Conjuncture." *IPPR Progressive Review* 24 (1): 36–44.

Fox, J. E., L. Moraşanu, and E. Szilassy. 2012. "The Racialization of the New European Migration to the UK." *Sociology* 46 (4): 680–695.

Gilroy, P. [1987] 2002. *There Ain't No Black in the Union Jack*. London: Routledge.

Gilroy, P. 2004. *After Empire: Melancholia or Convivial Culture?* Abingdon: Routledge.

Gilroy, P. 2019. "Still No Black in the Union Jack?" *Tribune*, January 26. https://www.tribunemag.co.uk/2019/01/still-no-black-in-the-union-jack.

Gilroy, P., T. Sandset, S. Bangstad, and Gard Ringen Højberg. 2019. "A Diagnosis of Contemporary Forms of Racism, Race and Nationalism: a Conversation with Professor Paul Gilroy." *Cultural Studies* 33 (2): 173–197.

Gramsci, A. [1930] 2011. *Prison Notebooks: Volume 2*. New York: Columbia University Press.

Gray, J. 2010. "Thatcher, Thatcher, Thatcher." *London Review of Books* 32 (8): 19–21.

Gupta, S., and S. Virdee. 2018. "European Crises: Contemporary Nationalisms and the Language of 'Race'." *Ethnic and Racial Studies* 41 (10): 1747–1764.

Hage, G. 2017. *Is Racism an Environmental Threat?* London: Polity Press.

Hall, S. 1979. "The Great Moving Right Show." *Marxism Today*, January, 14–20.

Hall, S. 1992. "The West and the Rest: Discourse and Power." In *Formations of Modernity*, edited by S. Hall, and B. Gieben, 185–227. London: Polity Press.

Hall, S. 1996. "Who Needs 'Identity'?" In *Questions of Cultural Identity*, edited by S. Hall and P. Du Gay, 1–17. London: Sage.

Hall, S. 2018. *Essential Essays, Volume 1: Foundations of Cultural Studies*. Durham, NC: Duke University Press.

Hall, S., C. Critcher, T. Jefferson, J. Clarke, and B. Roberts. [1978] 2013. *Policing the Crisis: Mugging, the State, and Law & Order*. London: Red Globe Press.

Hardt, M., and A. Negri. 2000. *Empire*. Cambridge, MA: Harvard University Press.

Henley, J. 2019. "Denmark's Centre-Left Set to Win Election with Anti-Immigration Shift." *Guardian*, June 4. https://www.theguardian.com/world/2019/jun/04/denmark-centre-left-predicted-win-election-social-democrats-anti-immigration-policies.

James, M. 2018. "Authoritarian Populism/Populist Authoritarianism." In *Regeneration Songs: Sounds of Investment and Loss in East London*, edited by A. Duman, D. Hancox, M. James, and A. Minton, 291–306. London: Repeater.

James, M., and S. Valluvan. 2018. "Left Problems, Nationalism and the Crisis." *Salvage* 6: 165–174.

Jones, H., Y. Gunaratnam, G. Bhattacharyya, W. Davies, S. Dhaliwal, K. Forkert, E. Jackson, and R. Salthus. 2017. *Go Home? The Politics of Immigration Controversies*. Manchester: Manchester University Press.

Kapoor, N. 2019. "Citizenship Deprivation at the Nexus of Race, Gender and Geopolitics." *Verso Blog*, February 22. https://www.versobooks.com/blogs/4250-citizenship-deprivation-at-the-nexus-of-race-gender-and-geopolitics.

Kundnani, A. 2007. *The End of Tolerance*. London: Pluto Press.

Kwarteng, K., P. Patel, D. Raab, C. Skidmore, and E. Truss. 2012. *Britannia Unchained: Global Lessons for Growth and Prosperity*. Basingstoke: Palgrave Macmillan.

Leddy-Owen, C. 2019. *Nationalism, Inequality and England's Political Predicament*. Abingdon: Routledge.

Luyendijk, J. 2017. "No Wonder John Redwood Backs Brexit: He Will Make Money Out of it, After All." *Guardian*, November 14. https://www.theguardian.com/commentisfree/2017/nov/14/john-redwood-brexit-money-britain-eu.

Malik, N. 2018. "Hillary Clinton's Chilling Pragmatism Gives the Far Right a Free Pass." *Guardian*, November 23. https://www.theguardian.com/commentisfree/2018/nov/23/hillary-clinton-populism-europe-immigration.

Mbembe, A. 2003. "Necropolitics." *Public Culture* 15 (1): 11–40.

Mbembe, A. 2018a. *Critique of Black Reason*. Durham, NC: Duke University Press.

Mbembe, A. 2018b. "The Idea of a Borderless World." *Africa is a Country*, November 11. https://africasacountry.com/2018/11/the-idea-of-a-borderless-world.

McGhee, D. 2008. *The End of Multiculturalism?* Maidenhead: Open University Press.

Miles, R. 1982. *Racism and Migrant Labour*. London: Routledge and Kegan Paul.

Mirowski, P., and D. Plehwe. 2009. *The Road From Mont Pèlerin: the Making of the Neoliberal Thought Collective*. Cambridge, MA: Harvard University Press.

Mondon, A., and A. Winter. 2017. "Articulations of Islamophobia: From the Extreme to the Mainstream?" *Ethnic and Racial Studies* 40 (13): 2151–2179.

Mouffe, C. 2018. *For a Left Populism*. London: Verso.

Nagle, A. 2018. "The Left Case Against Open Borders." *American Affairs* 2: 4. https://americanaffairsjournal.org/2018/11/the-left-case-against-open-borders/.

Narayan, J. 2017. "The Wages of Whiteness in the Absence of Wages: Racial Capitalism, Reactionary Intercommunalism and the Rise of Trumpism." *Third World Quarterly* 38 (11): 2482–2500.

Norris, P., and R. Inglehart. 2019. *Cultural Backlash: Trump, Brexit and Authoritarian Populism*. Cambridge: Cambridge University Press.

O'Toole, F. 2018. *Heroic Failure: Brexit and the Politics of Pain*. London: Head of Zeus.

Said, E. [1978] 2003. *Orientalism*. London: Penguin Books.

Sayer, D. 2017. "White Riot - Brexit, Trump, and Post-factual Politics." *Historical Sociology* 30 (1): 90–106.

Shilliam, R. 2018. *Race and the Undeserving Poor*. Newcastle upon Tyne: Agenda Publishing.

Toscano, A. 2017. "Notes on Late Fascism." *Historical Materialism*, April 2. http://www.historicalmaterialism.org/blog/notes-late-fascism.

Trilling, D. 2019. *Lights in the Distance: Exile and Refuge at the Borders of Europe*. London: Verso.

Valluvan, S. 2019. *The Clamour of Nationalism*. Manchester: Manchester University Press.

Virdee, S., and B. McGeever. 2018. "Racism, Crisis, Brexit." *Ethnic and Racial Studies* 41 (10): 1802–1819.

Yuval-Davis, N. 2006. "Belonging and the Politics of Belonging." *Patterns of Prejudice* 40 (3): 197–214.

Yuval-Davis, N., G. Wemyss, and K. Cassidy. 2018. "Everyday Bordering, Belonging and the Reorientation of British Immigration Legislation." *Sociology* 52 (2): 228–244.

Deportation, racism and multi-status Britain: immigration control and the production of race in the present

Luke de Noronha

ABSTRACT
In this paper, I examine the experiences of Jason and Ricardo, two men who were deported to Jamaica from the UK following criminal conviction. This ethnographic inquiry into deportation provides a rich and complex account of race-making at different scales. Theorizing the connections between racialization and illegalization offers a productive framework for the study of racism in multi-status Britain. The paper argues that the border is central to race's contemporary mobilization, not only in the lives of individuals like Jason and Ricardo but also for those interpellated as "natives".

Introduction

In the spring of 2018 the so-called "Windrush scandal" erupted in the UK. It was discovered that people who had moved from the Caribbean before 1973 – "Commonwealth subjects" who should have had indefinite leave to remain – were being caught up in the UK's "hostile environment" immigration policy.[1] Amelia Gentleman at the Guardian, along with a few others, began to collect stories of people who had lost their jobs, houses, and access to health-care because they had been illegalized. The story picked up steam, leading to the resignation of Home Secretary Amber Rudd (Gentleman 2018). Quite quickly, a broad consensus emerged: the "Windrush generation" were citizens, members of the national "we", and as such their treatment had been unaccep-table and cruel. Crucially, the "Windrush generation" were not "illegal immi-grants", a group that both main political parties continued to characterize as undesirable and unwanted.

Importantly, the "Windrush scandal" allowed politicians and tabloid journalists to demonstrate that controls on immigration were not about race. By expressing sympathy with black "Windrush migrants", who belonged, and by contrasting them with "illegal immigrants", who did not, it was possible for commentators to claim that immigrants are judged on their "integration" and their conduct, and not on their race. As Bridget Anderson put it somewhat earlier:

> The prevailing contemporary logic seems to be that 'we' still do not like 'migrants', that migrants are now often white since they come from Europe and that 'we' includes Black people; therefore, it is not racist to say that we do not like migrants (Anderson 2015, 2).

The claim that the exclusion of immigrants has nothing to do with race is central to the justification for bordering in contemporary Britain. In this political context, it is important to re-theorize the connection between migration and race (Erel, Murji, and Nahaboo 2016). In this paper, I dispute the claim that the UK's immigration regime is somehow non-racist, by demonstrating the centrality of immigration controls to the production and mobilization of racial meanings in the present. In so doing, a sharper appreciation of the connections between race, nation and the border emerges. In particular, I develop these arguments through an ethnographic engagement with the lives of two men, Jason and Ricardo, both of who moved to the UK as children and spent half their lives in Britain, before being deported to Jamaica following criminal conviction (indeed, they were on the same deportation charter flight in November 2014).

This paper begins with a set of arguments about academic approaches to the study of migration and race. I argue that developing an account of *illegalization* is necessary to reach a historically specific account of contemporary British racisms (De Genova 2002). I then put these arguments to work by describing Jason and Ricardo's experiences. Jason lived in the UK for over fifteen years with "no recourse to public funds", and his illegality trapped him in destitution. For Jason, race, class and status were lived through one another, and theorizing these interconnections is crucial if we want to better understand multi-status Britain. Like Jason, Ricardo was deported following many years of police surveillance and harassment, and I argue that racism within the criminal justice system increasingly has deportation consequences. However, beyond suggesting that deportation is enforced disproportionately, the broader argument is that the immigration regime shapes and produces racial meanings and racist practices in the present. In other words, deportation not only reflects British racisms but produces and mobilizes them (Knowles 2010; Fox, Moroşanu, and Szilassy 2012). I elaborate these arguments through a close engagement with Jason and Ricardo's experiences and interpretations.

Race in migration studies

Migration studies and ethnic and racial studies are now largely distinct disciplines within the British academy, but this has not always been so (Schuster 2010). In fact, it had previously been assumed that studies of race were, by default, studies of migration and migrants (Knowles 2010, 37; Erel, Murji, and Nahaboo 2016, 1339). In the 60s, 70s and 80s, Britain's "ethnic minorities" were mostly postwar migrants and their descendants, and so studies of race and ethnicity *implied* immigration. Moreover, the politics of immigration and the politics of race were thoroughly imbricated in public debates – in that "immigration" meant "coloured immigration" and black and brown Britons were, and are, defined as second and third generation migrants (Gilroy 1987). When returning to earlier work on race and racism, it is worth bearing this in mind:

> This is not a crisis of race. But race punctuates and periodizes the crisis. Race is the lens through which people come to perceive that a crisis is developing. It is the framework though which the crisis is experienced. It is the means by which the crisis is to be resolved – 'send it away' (Hall 1978, 31–32).

Stuart Hall's analysis of race here implies immigration. I would even suggest that the word "race" could be replaced with the word "immigration" in the quote above, and it would still retain much of its original meaning. "Send it away" might imply incarceration (i.e. law and order), but it might also suggest repatriation, which has been one central rallying call of British racist expression throughout the postwar years (indeed, the pervasiveness of that familiar racist refrain, "go back to your country", is one of the key reasons that deportation offers such a critical lens onto British racism).

This is not a call to romanticize the ethnic and racial studies of yesteryear – immigration and race were conceived of very differently by scholars working with different approaches – and this remains the case. Erel, Murji, and Nahaboo (2016, 1339) provide a helpful "framework for understanding how race is conceptualized (or ignored) in contemporary scholarship on migration", noting the diverse ways in which scholars working in different traditions theorize the race-migration nexus. In their conclusion, they argue that approaches to the study of migration which eschew race and racialization analytically, while presenting racism as somehow external to European identity, work to deny the necessity of anti-racist approaches to migration, approaches which are especially urgent in the context of Europe's border crisis and broad political shifts to the (far) right.

For Lentin (2014), mainstream European migration studies is "epistemically racist" and thus complicit with the postracial deflections, denials and dismissals which obscure Europe's colonial histories and the ongoing vitality of racist culture. Liberal migration studies is often preoccupied with "integration"

– operationalized in terms of migrants and minorities identifying with the "host country", speaking the language, and displaying "interethnic social contacts" (see e.g. Ersanilli & Koopmans 2010). Colonial histories and global disparities fade from view, and questions about racism are recast in terms of "hostility towards out-groups" and "ethnic segregationism", which of course work both ways (Koopmans 2010, 2015). These approaches to migration problematize "migrants and minorities" rather than borders, and their proponents are some of the most prominent and well-funded migration researchers in Europe. The landscape in the British academy does differ significantly from countries like the Netherlands, France or Germany (Schuster 2010), but "raceless" and policy-friendly approaches to studying "migrants and minorities" have become popular (Alexander 2018). Superdiversity represents one such analytic.

'Diversity in Britain is not what it used to be', Steven Vertovec (2007) argues in the first line of his widely cited superdiversity article (indeed, the most widely read article in this journal). Vertovec might be right to identify new kinds of complexity and difference, but his framing remains wholly descriptive, his conception of diversity arithmetic, and his ignorance of 'close to 30 years of scholarship on the relationship between racism and urban multiculture' palpable (Back and Sinha 2016, 520). These critiques have been well made elsewhere (Claire Alexander refers to the 'empty empiricisms of superdiversity', for example (2018, 1044)).

That said, Vertovec does point to the importance of different immigration statuses that carry "quite specific and legally enforceable entitlements, controls, conditions and limitations" (2007, 1036), and this insight is important. Vertovec lists several different migration statuses (e.g. workers, students, spouses, asylum seekers, irregular migrants), and then suggests that immigration status fractures ethnicity, and has consequences for, amongst other things, how people relate to labour markets. While this is helpful, it remains conceptually flat, failing to work theoretically and politically beyond this fairly dry, even if kaleidoscopic, empirical observation (see Kofman (2002) and Morris (2003) for earlier accounts which provide more productive accounts of legal status).

It is preferable, therefore, to examine processes of *illegalization*. Rather than reifying immigration status, it is the state's power to actively illegalize non-citizens through legal categorization and coercive power that should be the central object of scrutiny (De Genova 2002). In this light, immigration status is not simply another social variable which crosscuts or intersects others, but the product of state processes which classify, exclude and separate. It is these processes of exclusion and illegalization, as they interact with experiences of racism and multiculture, that should the focus of our critical inquiries (see Back and Sinha 2018). Indeed, exploring these processes of illegalization is especially important in contemporary Britain, because "everyday/

everywhere borders" have become increasingly central to public and political life (Yuval-Davis, Wemyss, and Cassidy 2017).

Between 1993 and 2015, the number of non-citizens living in the UK increased from around two million to over five million (Rienzo and Vargas-Silva 2017).[2] In recent years, the UK has allocated more resources to immigration enforcement – particularly targeting "illegal immigrants" within the "hostile environment" – and these policies have rendered non-EU citizens increasingly temporary and deportable. Whether because of immigration raids on homes and places of work, or because of the routine immigration checks now outsourced to landlords, teachers, and doctors, many non-citizens are increasingly hemmed in by the borders designed to identify and exclude them(Yuval-Davis, Wemyss, and Cassidy 2017). It becomes important, therefore, to pay attention to how these myriad bordering practices in what I call *multi-status Britain* generate complementary shifts in meanings and experiences that are specifically racialised in form. Following De Genova, I am concerned here with the relationship between racialization and illegalization in multi-status Britain (De Genova 2005).

Arguably, however, multi-status is simply a synonym for superdiverse. That may be so, but my intention in describing Britain as multi-status is to draw attention to the law, enforcement and exclusion – always in relation to race, racism and racialization – in a way which offers a more productive analytic than "diversity". It is not simply, as Vertovec puts it, that being a "student", "spouse", "worker", "asylum seeker" or "undocumented migrant" produces new configurations of "diversity", but much more importantly that these juridical categories produce multifaceted exclusions (De Genova 2002). By defining Britain as multi-*status*, I am centring the border. Borders "have been transported to the middle of political space", and are "implosive, infinitely elastic, and, in effect, truly everywhere *within* the space of the nation-state" (Balibar 2004: 104); borders produce "tensions between access and denial, mobility and immobilization, discipline and punishment, freedom and control" (Casas-Cortes et al. 2015, 57). On this account, bordering practices produce a range of legal statuses and social positionings which fundamentally concern questions of power, inequality and state violence. It is this kind of critical perspective which is lacking where diversity provides the optic.

By theorizing Britain as multi-status, then, I am arguing that immigration control should be central to any account of social inequality in contemporary Britain, and to theorisations of race and racism in particular. Indeed, the prefix "multi" has been used in several debates about race in Britain – the UK has variously been described as multi-ethnic, multi-cultural, multi-racial, multi-racist, and characterized by emergent forms of multiculture – and defining the UK as multi-status is intended to centre immigration control within broader conversations about race, nationalism and culture.

The border in ethnic and racial studies

The critique of migration studies so far has been necessarily broad-brush, and it should not be read as an outright dismissal of some coherent body of work we might call "migration studies" (see Erel, Murji, and Nahaboo 2016). In fact, my intention in this piece is also to identify the paucity of theorisations of the border within ethnic and racial studies. Put simply, the problem is equally that many scholars of race and racism have failed to think substantively about legal status, bordering and citizenship/alienage. Returning to prominent theorisations of race, nation and multiculture in Britain – particularly the work of Paul Gilroy (1987, 2004) – immigration is often defined as the central public issue and theme that organizes defensive conceptions of the racial nation. However, among scholars who work with these insights, such claims are not always actively connected to the actual material and legal differences in status that shape the experiences of young "black Britons".

With the intensification of internal borders and the deepening exclusions facing non-citizens, many multi-ethnic groups of young people today are divided by immigration and citizenship status, whether they talk about it or not. I am therefore suggesting that studies of racism and multiculture in urban Britain should be examining questions of belonging in legal as much as cultural terms, examining the weight of legal categorisations in the formation of identities. Immigration controls create "new hierarchies of belonging" (Back and Sinha 2018), and Britain's multi-status character complicates how we think about and study race and racism, particularly when discussing issues of citizenship, belonging and identity.

If the critique of mainstream migration studies is that there has been a limited account of race, racism and state power, then the critique of ethnic and racial studies is that as border regimes have become more complex, internalized and heavily enforced, there has been a lack of scholarly attention to their specific operation and consequences. This is arguably reflective of the wider absence of theorisations of the state following the cultural turn in ethnic and racial studies (Goldberg 2002), and my argument is that focusing on immigration control provides an important means of theorizing historically specific racisms in ways which centre the state (Hall 1980). Crucially, this is not a call to marginalize analyses of discourse and culture. It is rather a claim to recover a more appropriate balance, one which provides attentiveness to the state, the law, and to the material conditions and consequences of everyday/everywhere bordering.

One productive line of inquiry, in this regard, is to theorize the ways in which immigration controls actively produce race at different scales (Knowles 2010). Rather than uncovering racially discriminatory immigration enforcement practices, or reasserting the metonymic connection between immigration and race, both of which remain worthwhile, I am suggesting that immigration controls and citizenship restrictions themselves are productive of racial meanings and inequalities in the present. Racial distinctions are "the contingent outcome of immigration policy, practices, and processes", rather than existing *a priori* (Fox, Moroşanu, and Szilassy 2012, 692). While racist expressions do not emerge anew each day, racism is always historically specific (Hall 1980), and border regimes are central to the production, or reconfiguration, of race as a social relation and system of difference.

In sum, critical accounts of race and nation in Britain need to attend to bordering practices. In what follows, I will operationalize and ground these arguments ethnographically, particularly through analysing the experiences of two men, Jason and Ricardo, who arrived to the UK as children, and were deported to Jamaica, half their lives later, following interaction with the criminal justice system. I will analyse the connections between processes of racialization, criminalization and illegalization, as they played out in these men's lives, and will restate in more detail how such a framework is generative for broader studies of race and migration. Before introducing Jason and Ricardo however, I provide a brief account of my methodology.

Methodology

The study is based on ethnographic methods – prolonged contact, "deep hanging out", and participant observation – as well as life-story interview methods. The fieldwork for this ethnographic project was conducted over two years, from 2015–2017, including three trips to Jamaica totalling around seven months. I met and interviewed over fifty deported people, but came to know around ten deported people especially well. I conducted several life story interviews with each of my key interlocutors over the course of the fieldwork period, and spent many hours "hanging out" and having informal conversations. Between fieldwork trips in Jamaica, I was in the UK conducting research with friends and family members of the deported people I met in Jamaica.

The men in this ethnographic study were all defined as "foreign criminals" in British law. Since the "foreign prisoner crisis" of 2006 – a media-produced scandal concerning the release of "foreign offenders", following which the Home Office was declared "not fit for purpose" – non-citizens with criminal records have been prioritized in Home Office deportation drives (Kaufman 2015). Several changes to law, policy and practice have expedited their removal. The overall effect of these multiple, interacting legal changes has been to lower the threshold for "criminality", to restrict the weight accorded to family ties and years spent in the UK, and to deny "foreign offenders" access to appeal rights. This expendability renders the study of "foreign criminals" particularly productive when examining the normative content of contemporary citizenship.

28   RACIAL NATIONALISMS

In this paper, I include accounts from two men from the larger study, Jason and Ricardo, both men who I have known for around three years and who I remain in regular contact with. While this is only a short paper and not a monograph, I want something of Jason and Ricardo's character to come through. I try to provide more than just "a bunch of disembodied thoughts that come out of subject's mouths" (Duneier and Back 2006, 554), and use descriptions and long quotes to this effect. My own view is that men like Jason and Ricardo have much to teach us about racism in contemporary Britain, and my theorisations on race and immigration control emerge out of sustained engagement, close listening and ongoing conversation with deported people like Jason and Ricardo.

Jason: race, class and status as mutually constitutive

I met Jason in 2015, on only my second day in Jamaica. I was spending the day down at the Salvation Army in Kingston, where the city's homeless come for food each day, when Jason bounded in at quite some pace, frenetic and loud. He spoke with a distinctly East London accent, and when I introduced myself my own accent clearly took him by surprise. "I'm from Manchester, yes", I explained. He was slightly manic, and told me about a young woman from Manchester that he had dated when he was in England. He brandished his Sondico trainers, a budget sports brand in the UK, and said "You know about Sondico, innit?!". He was full of life, charming and intense. We sat down for a while, and Jason explained that he was homeless, living in a shelter in East Kingston. He also spoke about his years in London, and how difficult it had been because he had "no ID". This was the first of many after-noons I spent with Jason, and as we got to know one another he spoke more about his years living homeless on the streets of London.

Jason left Jamaica when he was fifteen years old, to join his mother who had been living in London for twelve years. He found it difficult to get along with her and his step-father, and before long he had been "kicked out" of the house and was living on the streets. I asked Jason, "Did you not want to come back to Jamaica when you found England difficult?" "Of course I did", he replied, "but when I told my mum that I wanted to go back before the six-month visa expired, she said, 'are you mad?' And took my passport away from me". Jason's mum took his passport and "dashed it in the bin", and so his exclusion from family was knotted up with state controls on movement – the passport, the visa, the border. Jason was not allowed to move back to Jamaica, but neither would he be allowed to remain in Britain legally. When Jason was homeless, unable to claim benefits or work, his immediate family members – his mother, aunties and his cousins – were all on a path to British citizenship. Jason's exclusion from family, then, was always about his exclusion from British citizenship.

Jason spent many years homeless, often sleeping on buses or walking around the West End at night, trying to avoid the bitter cold of London's winters:

> Jason: Yeah. I literally slept in the cold on the streets one time, in ice. In ice my friend, you know. I padded up in somebody's doorway, at the back of their house in erm, Barking, near the bus station, yeah. Barking Bus station, and I padded up behind there and just had a sleep you know.

Jason learnt to survive without any state support, and in this context he had repeated run-ins with the police. As Jason explains, "The problem with my life was I've been in and out of police stations"; "my life was morely like being in handcuffs". Jason was mostly arrested for minor infractions, especially drunk and disorderly or not paying travel fares, but he also spent some time in prison, on remand, for several offences, including common assault, theft, damage to property and skipping bail. Importantly, Jason's experiences of criminalization can only be understood in direct relation to his destitution.

When Jason was homeless, he developed friendships with other homeless people, many of whom were British citizens. These homeless British citizens, at least nominally, had access to housing and welfare benefits. Clearly, however, British citizens fall into homelessness too, and increasingly so (Cooper and Whyte 2017). For poor and disadvantaged British citizens, the state is hollowing out their access to social rights, protections and welfare, while intensifying forms of punishment, criminalization and surveillance – both of which are driven by a kind of moral authoritarianism designed, in many instances, to discipline the poor into underpaid and insecure wage labour. This mode of government, this punishment of the poor, is what Wacquant describes as "neoliberal statecraft" (Wacquant 2009, 287–314). However, while rights to housing, education, and benefits are being eroded for all British citizens, illegalized migrants like Jason are excluded totally (they have "no recourse to public funds"). Further, while homeless British citizens are increasingly criminalized and incarcerated (Cooper and Whyte 2017), non-citizens experience the added threat of coercion through detention and deportation. What is true for homeless British citizens – that the state is simultaneously abandoning *and* punitive – is compounded for non-citizens who are also subject to immigration control. Deportability itself is the condition of experiencing the state in this way (see De Genova 2002). Carter refers to deportability as "the revocability of the promise of a future" (1997, 196), and Jason articulated this in terms of being unable to progress in life because he had "no ID":

> Luke: Did you worry about getting sent back though? When all this was happening with the police, did you think about the prospect of being back in Jamaica?
>
> Jason: Every day, every day. Every day because it was something where I was thinking to myself, I don't have no stamp out here official in England,

for me to try and move somewhere. I don't have nowhere where I can say, yeah, this is my home. Yeah? I don't have nowhere where I can say to a girl, hey, let me take you out for a drink.

Luke: But specifically, I mean, deportation. Did you think about Jamaica?

Jason: Yeah, I knew this was going to happen.

Luke: Did you?

Jason: Yeah, from very young, I knew from sixteen this was going to happen to me, no matter what I tried, I knew it was going to happen because that is the system. I looked at the system way ago, and remember, where I lived, I lived in Essex, so you have posh cunts who have a BMW X6 or an R8. And they're not driving slow, they're pressing gas. And you know, I knew, I can't compete against them. I don't have a chance. How can I have a chance? They're always going to beat me.

In this conversation, Jason responds to a question about his deportability by describing the "posh cunts" in Essex who were always going to "beat him", and he complains about being unable to "say to a girl, hey, let me take you out for a drink". Clearly, Jason's illegality was experienced in relation to class, gender and racial identity. Jason could not disentangle race from class and immigration status; they were lived through one another, and these connections demonstrate the need to incorporate immigration control into a wider analysis of social inequality in contemporary Britain.

These connections between race, class and status were particularly audible when Jason described his experiences of racism in the UK. He often spoke about harassment and abuse from the police, and he described many accounts of racist street violence. He spoke about being called a "black cunt" on public transport, about people hurling racist abuse at him from pub gardens, and about groups of white men attacking him in Essex, London and Wales. Jason explained these incidents of racist violence in terms of him being black, but also in terms of his poverty, or the fact that he looked poor:

Jason: You know, it was like, oh, this guy looks a bit dodgy. I'm not dodgy, and I wouldn't come across to a person dodgy, you know what I mean? I'm straight up and forward. But then when you have that look, you have a chipped tooth, you have a little cut on your face, people straight away, "oh you're a thug".

From Jason's descriptions of racist events, and his feelings about how he was perceived, it is clear that race and class were mutually constitutive. It was having a chipped tooth that made Jason look like "a thug", just as it was looking like he lived on the street that led to him being arrested. Notably, Jason said that the police were racist, always watching and harassing him, but he always related this to his destitution and hypervisibilty:

Jason: I had a lot of run ins with the police, you know, and every time I was trying to avoid the attention, you know, they knew I was on the street, and you know, it was really hard. It was really hard because all you're trying to not get in trouble,

RACIAL NATIONALISMS

once you're on the street you're going to get in trouble. Understand, it's not somebody driving by and saying, oh, he's going about his business. It's the police, who is that? I see him last week, I see him again this week. Yes. And that's what was happening.

While racist discrimination from the police and racist violence from white men on the streets were profoundly distressing for Jason, they were experienced in relation to his material vulnerabilities as street homeless. For Jason, his illegality and homelessness were paramount because while he could navigate racist violence, he was trapped in destitution. Jason's destitution (his class location) was produced by immigration control. In fact, Jason makes this connection himself when he moves, in his own rather fluid way, from discussing racist violence to bemoaning his lack of immigration status:

> Jason: Some of the areas that I went to in Romford like Collier Row, and erm, Howard Hill, is very racial. So for you to go down there as a black person, you're not accepted, and it was really worrying in a state that you're living in the year 2000 and there's people out there still like that, that wouldn't mind head-butting others in the head, or burning down somebody's fuckin' house because there's Chinese living in there, or Nigerians living in there you nar mean, so, all round I, I faced a lot of difficulties pursuing that effect. But in terms of effect where I wanted to do me, that was much harder. Because I didn't have no right abode, address, yeah, I didn't have no ID, specialising me to move about somewhere, you know and, it was harder for me to get things, like job centre, post office ID, you know? So I've said to myself, erm, let me try and do something, but I was on the street.

When Jason connects acts of racist violence in a "very racial area" to his own experiences of illegality, he reveals the connections he makes between different modes of exclusion. Following Jason's own meandering narrative, his main issue was not having ID, and the rightlessness and abjection which flowed from that, which rendered him more vulnerable to various kinds of racist harassment and violence. Jason's experiences and his own reflections allow for a sharper acknowledgement of how race, class *and* legal status are mutually constitutive, and inextricably so. This is true at different scales: within Jason's own biography, in immigration regimes more broadly, and in a racialised world of unequal and bordered nation-states. This argument connects local acts of street and state racism – which might otherwise be defined only in terms of discrimination, prejudice and "hate crime" – to the legal borders of citizenship. Ricardo's story allows me to pursue this argument from another direction.

Ricardo: race-making at the border

I met Ricardo in Montego Bay, Jamaica's second city, around a year after he had been returned. He was struggling to adjust to life in Jamaica, and felt unsafe in an unfamiliar city, particularly because his older brother, who had also been deported from the UK, was murdered in Montego Bay two years earlier. Ricardo moved to the UK when he was ten-years-old and went to school in the West Midlands. I asked him about growing up in the UK and he described his interactions with the police, explaining that he had been arrested over one-hundred times, and always released without charge. His experiences with the police were so extreme, and so important to the questions that had led me to Jamaica, that I kept returning to them. I encouraged Ricardo to transport me back to his life as a sixteen-year-old, when clad in all "black garms" he had to work out how to see his friends without getting arrested and spending hours in a police cell.

Ricardo explained that between the ages of fifteen and eighteen he was "just always getting arrested for robberies". He began to feel that he could not leave his house without being harassed and arrested by the police. To be clear, Ricardo said that he had never committed a robbery, and yet was repeatedly arrested, interrogated and then released without charge. Often the police would show him some CCTV footage, claiming that the person on screen was wearing his clothes, trainers, or displayed his body comportment. Ricardo said that many of these accusations were laughable, when the person on camera looked nothing like him and was committing an offence somewhere he had never been.

When Ricardo was sixteen and seventeen, he started staying at home to avoid the police. Because he was "known to the police for robberies", despite never having been charged with an offence, he was assigned a personal officer, PC Marsden, a name neither he nor his friends had forgotten. PC Marsden would come and check on Ricardo, daily, to record whether he was in and what he was wearing: "Most of the time I'd just go down in my boxers and my socks, because they just write down what you're wearing, because of the matching description bit". When Ricardo left his house he would often see PC Marsden, waiting for him and his friends: "He's always on the bike, bicycle, he would just ride around and wait for us to come out, and follow us and just say 'where you guys going, you going to rob someone today?'"

The police also set up a camera directly outside Ricardo's house, which faced their front door, apparently to combat "anti-social behaviour". Ricardo and his friends told me that the police used to "kick the front door in" when looking for his brother, and "the door was always broken", the lock unable to catch. Ricardo was harassed almost whenever he left the house, arrested countless times and taken to the police station; he was denied access to public space, to freedom of association, and to the presumption of innocence.

Importantly, Ricardo's experiences are not atypical. Most deportees I met in Jamaica described racist policing practices. This does not mean they were not engaged in criminal acts, only that they were more likely to be caught, arrested, charged and convicted (see Lammy 2017). Of course, these kinds of heavy and disproportionate policing practices have consequences for which non-citizens are vulnerable to deportation power. Experiences of racism, particularly at the hands of the police, mean that citizenship's internal exclusions are mapped onto the border. Put differently, the nation is policed in ways which are not directly about controlling immigration – i.e. street and police racism – and yet which inevitably have consequences for who is most vulnerable to illegalization and deportation. For example, Australian overstayers working in bars simply do not experience the institutions of policing and immigration enforcement in the same way as racialised non-citizens like Ricardo and Jason, even as, in law, the Australian overstayer is an "illegal immigrant" too. In a context in which there are more "illegal immigrants" than can be deported – what Matthew Gibney (2008) refers to as "the deportation gap" – racial discrimination within state institutions has consequences for which non-citizens are likely to have their status as non-members realized.

My argument, however, is not restricted to the claim that racist discrimination determines who is most likely to be deported. I am also concerned with mapping the processes through which race is made, and immigration controls not only reflect ideas about "racialised outsiders" but also reconfigure them (Virdee 2014). The fact that borders produce racial meanings became especially clear when I met Ricardo's best friend, Melissa, and she shared one particular anecdote with me.

> Melissa: Yeah it was exactly like that, everywhere you walked, you'd get stopped, and it's like why you stopping us for? I remember one time, I got a mate who's Albanian, police man come over and was like, "you think you're black don't you mate". And then we're like "what"? And he's like, "remember you ain't even got a visa". This is what he's saying to the boy, and I'm just like hold your tongue, he wants you to say something to him. Don't say nothing, just walk off and stuff. Like, that's how police was round there.

In Melissa's account, immigration control is invoked directly by a police officer, "remember you ain't even got a visa", which demonstrates that immigration control produces new narratives on and targets for popular and police racism. Discourses on immigration at the national level permeate society, and get mobilized in local interactions, like in the instance Melissa related. This is also manifest in relation to emergent forms of racist violence targeting Eastern Europeans (Fox, Moroşanu, and Szilassy 2012), and "asylum seekers" and "refugees" (Schuster 2010). The targets of Home Office policy and street racism are invariably in dialogue; "racialised outsiders" take form at the border.

Clearly, immigration controls shape how racism gets expressed and articulated. This is apparent when a police officer invokes the lack of a visa, or when "asylum seekers" are attacked *qua* "asylum seekers". As important, however, are the more local encounters with immigration control which shape how people living in Britain understand race and (non)belonging. Let us consider the police officers who surveilled and harassed Ricardo throughout his teenage years. They are likely to be aware that he was deported post-sentence. Ricardo described familiar police officers attending his criminal trial and waving mockingly when he was convicted, and there was clearly a level of intimacy to their repeated encounters over the years. Those police officers denied Ricardo the right to space, mobility and the presumption of innocence – fundamental rights of citizenship – however, by virtue of his status, he was in fact not entitled to those rights of citizenship. Arguably, these police officers were vindicated by Ricardo's deportation, and their discriminatory policing practices were sanctioned by the exclusionary and expulsive logic of immigration control. Home Office policy and policing practices, then, are also inevitably in dialogue, and this is reinforced by specific institutional arrangements which marry policing work with bordering functions (see Parmar 2018).

Under a policy called "Operation Nexus", police officers in the UK now work with immigration officials to develop cases against non-citizens (Griffiths 2017). In particular, non-citizens who have not been convicted in criminal courts can still be deported based on "non-convictions" and police intelligence. In these cases, the police regularly provide witness statements and live evidence to the immigration tribunal, often alleging "gang involvement" (which is especially likely to affect Jamaican nationals). Thus, the police are actively involved in deportation processes, and the policing of "gangs" is now connected to and integrated within the deportation regime. This is particularly striking in a context in which the vast majority of those defined as "gang members" are young black men, despite young white men committing the vast majority of serious youth violence (see Williams and Clarke 2016 for stark statistics on this point). This co-construction of illegality and criminality through emergent institutional relationships between the police and immigration authorities has consequences for how racist criminal justice is to be understood in multi-status Britain.

Crucially, these kinds of practices point to something more than "disproportionality". Deportation not only reflects racist discrimination at an earlier stage but actively shifts how racism gets articulated thereafter. Put another way, it is not that Ricardo was racialised as black, criminalized as a result, and then subsequently illegalized, but rather that each set of processes feeds into the other. Ricardo's racialization as black is not fixed or static, reducible to skin colour, but works through his criminalization and illegalization. Further, localized racist encounters can only be understood in relation to the nativist anti-immigrant politics which is negotiated at the border. Race does not precede immigration control; race is always *in formation* (Knowles 2010), and illegality, criminality and blackness all confirm one another for people like Ricardo. This way of theorizing race better connects local acts of racist violence to the borders of citizenship.

Similarly, when Jason was called a "black cunt" and chased by a group of white men, we might conceive of this as a form of *bordering*. As Anoop Nayak argues: "the micro-politics of race hate that occurs in everyday encounters at a local scale can perform as a means of purging the nation and exerting white territoriality" (2017, 290). For my purposes, the "micro-politics of race hate" are intimately connected to exclusive citizenship regimes and the legal borders of the nation. Racist street violence and immigration controls are both forms of bordering which feed off one another. Again, this is about interpreting local manifestations of racism in relation to the broader demarcation of the national community through bordering. The challenge, however, is in refining our ability to move between scales and develop a coherent argument about the connections between localized racist encounters, national immigration policies, and global citizenship regimes.

In this paper, I have tried to connect localized instances of racist violence to the structuring force of citizenship and immigration law. This helps analyse processes of race-making in multi-status Britain, connecting the intimate and everyday to the structural, legal and institutional. Jason and Ricardo's experiences demonstrate that immigration controls structure various forms of racist expression and exclusion, providing both meaning and license to acts of nativist exclusion. Ultimately, I hope to have demonstrated that it is through close attention to the biographies of people like Jason and Ricardo that racism in multi-status Britain can best be theorized.

Conclusion

The politics of immigration is central to the mobilization of race in contemporary Britain. This is certainly true at the discursive level – the figure of the immigrant is part of the very intellectual mechanism that keeps us hostage (Gilroy 2004, 165) – but it is also true in relation to the law and its productive power in institutional and everyday life. In this article, I have tried to demonstrate how an ethnographic inquiry into specific immigration controls can provide a rich and complex account of race-making at different scales. Theorizing the connections between racialization and illegalization offers a generative framework for the study of race and racism in multi-status Britain.

Central to my argument is the claim that bordering practices and immigration regimes actively produce race. For Jason, race, class and status were lived through one another, and this demands that we trace processes of illegalization in relation to other social dynamics and inequalities. When discussing Ricardo's experiences, I argued that not only does racist policing have disproportionate deportation consequences, but that immigration controls themselves shape and reconfigure how discriminatory policing practices take form thereafter. Crucially, immigration controls make race meaningful, and this is true for young people growing up without status – and their friends and families – but also for British citizens who are interpellated as "natives". For police officers and street racists, it is in relation to the immigration regime that "racialised outsiders" often take form. Race is negotiated at the border.

Most importantly, it is through this kind of long term ethnographic engagement that it becomes possible to "bear witness" to the violence of immigration control, as lived by people like Jason and Ricardo. They both faced some of the most extreme manifestations of British state racism, and they are now struggling to rebuild their lives in Jamaica, far from home, their patois unconvincing and their "Britishness" hypervisible. By reflecting on their stories, we can develop new replies to those facile claims that controls on immigration have nothing to do with racism, ultimately so that we might develop a vital and astute anti-racism fit for these anti-immigrant times.

Notes

1. The current prime minister, Theresa May, introduced a range of policies when she was Home Secretary designed to create, and I quote, "a really hostile environment for illegal immigrants" (Travis 2013)
2. Importantly, nearly three million of these five million non-citizens are EU citizens, and their fate is unclear in light of the UK's impending exit from the European Union.

Disclosure Statement

No potential conflict of interest was reported by the author.

Funding

This work was supported by Economic and Social Research Council.

References

Alexander, C. 2018. "Breaking Black: the Death of Ethnic and Racial Studies in Britain." *Ethnic and Racial Studies* 41 (6): 1034–1054.

Anderson, B. 2015. "Book Review: Race, Gender and the Body in British Immigration Control: Subject by Examination." *British Journal of Criminology* 56 (1): 207–209.

Back, L., and S. Sinha. 2016. "Multicultural Conviviality in the Midst of Racism's Ruins." *Journal of Intercultural Studies* 37 (5): 517–532.

Back, L., and S. Sinha. 2018. *Migrant City*. London: Routledge.

Balibar, E. 2004. *We, the People of Europe?: Reflections on Transnational Citizenship*. Princeton, NJ: Princeton University Press.

Carter, D. 1997. *States of Grace: Senegalese in Italy and the New European Immigration*. Minneapolis: University of Minnesota Press.

Casas-Cortes, M., S. Cobarrubias, N. De Genova, G. Garelli, G. Grappi, C. Heller, S. Hess, et al. 2015. "New Keywords: Migration and Borders." *Cultural Studies* 29 (1): 55–87. doi:10.1080/09502386.2014.891630.

Cooper, V., and D. Whyte. 2017. *The Violence of Austerity*. London: Pluto Press.

De Genova, N. 2002. "Migrant "Illegality" and Deportability in Everyday Life." *Annual Review of Anthropology* 31 (1): 419–447.

De Genova, N. 2005. *Working the Boundaries: Race, Space, and "Illegality" in Mexican Chicago*. Durham, N.C.: Duke University Press.

Duneier, M., and L. Back. 2006. "Voices From the Sidewalk: Ethnography and Writing Race." *Ethnic and Racial Studies* 29 (3): 543–565.

Erel, U., K. Murji, and Z. Nahaboo. 2016. "Understanding the Contemporary Race-Migration Nexus." *Ethnic and Racial Studies* 39 (8): 1339–1360.

Ersanilli, E., and R. Koopmans. 2010. "Rewarding Integration? Citizenship Regulations and the Socio-Cultural Integration of Immigrants in the Netherlands, France and Germany." *Journal of Ethnic and Migration Studies* 36 (5): 773–791. doi:10.1080/1369183100376318.

Fox, J. E., L. Moroşanu, and E. Szilassy. 2012. "The Racialization of the New European Migration to the UK." *Sociology* 46 (4): 680–695.

Gentleman, A. 2018. Windrush victims voice shock at scandal's political consequences. *The Guardian*, May 1.

Gibney, M. 2008. "Asylum and the Expansion of Deportation in the United Kingdom." *Government and Opposition* 43 (2): 146–167.

Gilroy, P. 1987. *There Ain't No Black in the Union Jack*. London: Hutchinson.

Gilroy, P. 2004. *After Empire: Melancholia or Convivial Culture?* London: Routledge.

Goldberg, D. T. 2002. *The Racial State. Malden, Mass.* Oxford: Blackwell Publishers.

Griffiths, M. 2017. "Foreign, Criminal: a Doubly Damned Modern British Folk-Devil." *Citizenship Studies* 21 (5): 527–546.

Hall, S. 1978. *Racism and Reaction. In Five Views of Multi-Racial Britain*. London: Commission for Racial Equality.

Hall, S. 1980. "Race, Articulation and Societies Structured in Dominance." In *Black British Cultural Studies: A Reader*, edited by H. Baker, M. Diawara, and R. Lindeborg, 16–60. Chicago: University of Chicago Press.

Kaufman, E. 2015. *Punish and Expel: Border Control, Nationalism, and the new Purpose of the Prison*. Oxford: Oxford University Press.

Knowles, C. 2010. ""Theorizing Race and Ethnicity: Contemporary Paradigms and Perspectives"." In *The SAGE Handbook of Race and Ethnic Studies*, edited by P. Hill Collins, and J. Solomos, 23–42. Los Angeles: SAGE.

Kofman, E. 2002. "Contemporary European Migrations, Civic Stratification and Citizenship." *Political Geography* 21 (8): 1035–1054.

Koopmans, R. 2010. "Trade-Offs between Equality and Difference: Immigrant Integration, Multiculturalism and the Welfare State in Cross-National Perspective." *Journal of Ethnic and Migration Studies* 36 (1): 1–26. doi:10.1080/13691830903250881.

Koopmans, R. 2015. "Religious Fundamentalism and Hostility against Out-groups: A Comparison of Muslims and Christians in Western Europe". *Journal of Ethnic and Migration Studies* 41 (1): 33–57. doi:10.1080/1369183X.2014.935307.

Lammy, D. 2017. *The Lammy Review: An Independent Review Into the Treatment of, and Outcomes for, Black, Asian and Minority Ethnic Individuals in the Criminal Justice System*. London: Department of Justice.

Lentin, A. 2014. "Postracial Silences: The Othering of Race in Europe." In *Racism and Sociology*, edited by W. Hund, and A. Lentin, 69–104. Berlin: Lit Verlag.

Morris, L. 2003. *Managing Migration: Civic Stratification and Migrants' Rights*. London: Routledge.

Nayak, A. 2017. "Purging the Nation: Race, Conviviality and Embodied Encounters in the Lives of British Bangladeshi Muslim Young Women." *Transactions of the Institute of British Geographers* 42 (2): 289–302.

Parmar, A. 2018. "Policing Belonging: Race and Nation in the UK." In *Race, Criminal Justice and Migration Control: Enforcing the Boundaries of Belonging*, edited by M. Bosworth, A. Parmar, and Y. Vazquez, 108–126. Oxford: University of Oxford Press.

Rienzo, C., and C. Vargas-Silva. 2017. *Migrants in the UK: An Overview. Migration Observatory Briefing*. Oxford: COMPAS, University of Oxford.

Schuster, L. 2010. "Globalization, Migration and Citizenship." In *The Sage Handbook of Race and Ethnic Studies*, edited by J. Solomos, and P. H. Collins, 332–350. London: Sage.

Travis, A. 2013. Immigration bill: Theresa May defends plans to create 'hostile environment'. *The Guardian*, Oct 10.

Vertovec, S. 2007. "Super-diversity and its Implications." *Ethnic and Racial Studies* 30 (6): 1024–1054.

Virdee, S. 2014. *Racism, Class and the Racialized Outsider*. Basingstoke: Palgrave MacMillan.

Wacquant, L. 2009. *Punishing the Poor: the Neoliberal Government of Social Insecurity*. Durham, NC: Duke University Press.

Williams, P., and B. Clarke. 2016. *Dangerous Associations: Joint Enterprise, Gangs and Racism. Centre for Crime and Justice Studies*. London: Centre for Crime and Justice Studies.

Yuval-Davis, N., G. Wemyss, and K. Cassidy. 2017. "Everyday Bordering, Belonging and the Reorientation of British Immigration Legislation." *Sociology* 52 (2): 228–244. doi:10.1177/0038038517702599.

More in common: the domestication of misogynist white supremacy and the assassination of Jo Cox

Hannah Jones ⓘ

ABSTRACT
This article considers responses to the murder of a British Member of Parliament, Jo Cox, in June 2016. Cox, a white woman, was assassinated by a white supremacist whose violent hatred extended to white people he deemed "collaborators" and who also exhibited strong misogyny. Cox is remembered for the message in her first speech to Parliament ("we have more in common than that which divides us") and a "More in Common" campaign was established in her memory. The article situates Cox's assassination alongside other recent attacks on female, feminist, and racially minoritized political leaders in the UK. Considering feminist and colonial resonances of domestication, the article argues that while the message of "More in Common" holds appeal, the figuring of Cox as foremost a (white) wife and mother has prevented a political confrontation with the misogynist white supremacy of the society in which this violence occurs.

Introduction: a political assassination

In June 2016, Labour Member of Parliament, Jo Cox, was shot and stabbed to death in the street in her constituency of Batley and Spen in Yorkshire, a week before the UK's referendum on membership of the European Union. The man who killed her shouted "Britain First" and "Keep Britain independent," and was later found to have far-right literature in his house and to have been involved with white supremacist groups. He was tried for terrorism offences and, six months later, found guilty of murder and sentenced to a whole-life prison sentence, the crime deemed by the judge to have been "committed to advance a cause associated with Nazism" (Cobain and Taylor 2016).

This political assassination drew national and international attention, outrage, and sorrow. Those close to Cox were determined that the tragic and violent end to her life would not be used to undermine the values she

40 RACIAL NATIONALISMS

advocated. Her husband Brendan was instrumental in ensuring the message of Cox's maiden speech in the Houses of Parliament was central to remembering her. In it, she described her parliamentary constituency of Batley and Spen in West Yorkshire:

> It is a joy to represent such a diverse community. Batley and Spen is a gathering of typically independent, no-nonsense and proud Yorkshire towns and villages. Our communities have been deeply enhanced by immigration, be it of Irish Catholics across the constituency or of Muslims from Gujarat in India or from Pakistan, principally from Kashmir. While we celebrate our diversity, what surprises me time and time again as I travel around the constituency is that *we are far more united and have far more in common than that which divides us.* (Hansard 2015; emphasis added)

Mass gatherings in London, Batley and elsewhere in the week after her death (and before the EU referendum) came together under the "More in Common" banner. Good wishes of sorrow and solidarity were sent from around the world, including from Barack Obama (Cox 2017). Brendan Cox characterized the attack as:

> a political act, an act of terrorism, but in the history of such acts it was perhaps the most incompetent and self-defeating. An act driven by hatred which instead has created an outpouring of love. (Cox 2017, 216).

This was based on a view that the murderer's motive was to create fear and division; therefore drawing people together (and against such acts) was seen as a healing gesture, in line with Cox's ethos. The More in Common campaign included establishing a charitable foundation in Cox's name to focus on her political priorities of loneliness, the Syrian conflict, women in public life and civilians in conflict (Jo Cox Foundation, n.d.); and a day of public street parties and picnics under the banner "The Great Get Together". Other initiatives in her memory include a leadership programme for women in the Labour Party, a fund named after her by the Department for International Development, an annual memorial lecture at the University of Cambridge, the renaming of *Rue Jo Cox* in Avallon, France and *Place Jo Cox* in Brussels, and a plaque in the House of Commons. Brendan Cox published a book about his wife's life and death entitled *More in Common* (Cox 2017).

My argument in this article is that the More in Common response is insufficient and counterproductive in terms of countering white supremacism. While values of "love and solidarity" are laudable, their articulation in this campaign reinforce a deeply gendered form of white nationhood. The response to the assassination of a national elected representative has been dampened in significance because of an appeal to her life as a wife and mother rather than as a political actor in her own right. This appeal does not deal with why and how this assassination happened – the political context – and therefore how such attacks could be countered. Through a focus on the domestic, the murder is imagined as a random, tragic occurrence. By figuring the assassination as an exceptional act by a "deranged individual" or "crazed loner", the underlying context of domesticated misogynist white supremacy in which his wilder expressions of those values could be incubated, is ignored. The response to the murder – though perhaps not intentionally – re-centres normative white patriarchal family values as essentially "British", whilst claiming to do the opposite. An alternative and more challenging approach would face head-on the roots of misogynist white supremacism in wider British society. It would also confront Cox's assassination as an extreme example of more widespread resistance to the increasing numbers of women and racially minoritized people gaining positions of power.

In this article, I refer to "white supremacy" in various registers. The man who murdered Cox can be straightforwardly regarded as a white supremacist given the documentation of his beliefs and associations; as *The Guardian* reported,

> Mair was racist and a terrorist in the making, his home stuffed with far-right books and Nazi memorabilia and his mind brimming with a belief that white people were facing an existential threat ... His greatest obsession, however, and his deepest bitterness was over those white people whom he condemned in his writings as "the collaborators": the liberals, the left and the media ... In the days before the murder he sought out information about the Ku Klux Klan, the Waffen SS, Israel, serial killers and matricide. (Cobain, Parveen, and Taylor 2016)

Central to this article's argument is that this extreme, virulent, overt, and mostly un-accepted white supremacism (and related misogyny) should not be separated in our analysis from the everyday white supremacism (and misogyny) which is embedded in British culture (Ahmed 2012). Everyday white supremacism is manifested: in the tendency of news media to immediately characterize violent attacks by people racialized as white as "lone wolf" or "mental health" issues, compared to an immediate identification of such acts by people identified as Muslim as "Islamic terrorism" (Freedman 2017); in the continuing normalization of everyday violence against people racialized as "of colour" (Gallagher and Winddance Twine 2017); in the ongoing understanding of whiteness as "the norm" which pervades our cultural codes and interactions (Du Bois [1920] 1969; Wekker 2016); and in the ways these racialized norms are intertwined and interdependent with the (racially differentiated) marginalization of women (Yuval-Davis 1993; Hill Collins 1998).

The distinction between "un-respectable" and "respectable" misogynist white supremacism might be considered the relationship between the "wild", "unruly", or "undomesticated" misogynist white supremacism of Cox's murderer on the one hand, and the "domesticating" and "domesticated" misogynist white supremacism of daily life on the other. I build on Ghassan Hage's writing on the domestication of difference and resistance inherent in nation-building multiculturalist projects. His analogy is with the domestication of animals by humans through which one asserts dominance over an absolute other. For me, the analogy is of domestic oppression within the home. This links the domination inherent in patriarchal home- and family-building, with the taming of "internal" struggles over power inequalities within the nation.

The article begins with a consideration of the relationship of home and nation in terms of the domestic, bringing together work from security studies, feminist theory, and post-colonial thinking to understand power in relation to rhetorical and material struggles over national belonging. This is followed by an exploration of the broader political context in which Cox was assassinated, demonstrating the pervasive nature of misogynist white supremacist feeling and actions in the UK. This involves an examination of the contradictions of ongoing nationally-professed commitments to equality – particularly gender equality – and how concern for equality can reproduce racialized gender relations, where both racism and sexism are imagined as "others" to "British values", thereby ignoring their ongoing operation within Britain (see e.g. Ahmed 2012). This is considered within and beyond the response to Cox's assassination and her memorialization as primarily a (dom-esticated) wife and mother concerned with her local community – occupying the space misogynist white supremacy would see as suitable for a young white woman. These everyday forms of misogynist white supremacy are linked to the rise of more extreme, undomesticated actions, particularly directed against women and racially minoritized people and their supporters – but most virulently against racially minoritized women – who are visible in national political life, demonstrating further that Cox's death was part of a pattern and not an isolated, random incident. I conclude by arguing that an alternative to "More in Common" would directly examine and challenge the misogynist white supremacism at the heart of our society.

Domestication, domopolitics: home, gender and nation

"Home" is commonly considered to be a place of safety and value. Yet there is an underside to the surface pleasantry of "home". The right to claim a place as "home" is frequently contested in the politics of nation and belonging, with the racist call of "Go Home" at once imagining a place where the person told to "go home" will be safe/welcome, and refusing that their current location could be their home (Jones et al. 2017). The safety and comfort of the more intimate home, too, has been questioned by feminists and sociol-ogists of the family (e.g. Barrett and McIntosh [1982] 2014). In this section, I consider the framing of domestication that will be used to understand the limitations of the dominant public response to Jo Cox's assassination.

In William Walters' (2004) analysis of the UK Home Office's 2001 White Paper, *Strong Borders, Safe Haven*, he identifies themes of nationhood and exclusion apparent in the New Labour statement of intent on immigration for its second term of government, following a significant rise in asylum claims in the UK (see also Yuval-Davis, Anthias, and Kofman 2005). Walters identifies a strain in governmental security regimes which he calls *domopolitics*, arguing this represents a shift from thinking about the nation as a household, towards thinking of it as a home. The emphasis, he suggests, moves from "an image of rule in which the state is conceived as a vast household requiring the wise stewardship of a patriarchal sovereign" (Walters 2004, 241) with rules to be made and obeyed, to a place of intimacy, belonging and feeling – a cosier, affective national belonging, but one where there remains a distinction between insiders and outsiders. The term "domopolitics" makes an etymological link with both forceful (domination, domestication) and cosy (domestic) resonances of home. Walters' emphasis is on how governments figure the "homeland" as at risk from unwanted intruders, and associate transnational movement as linked to threats (terrorism, criminality, unfair use of resources) to those "at home".

Though Walters references links with family, gender and race, these are not elaborated in his paper. The gendered nature of home, and how this translates through domopolitics, was more recently taken up by Gwyneth Lonergan (2018), to consider the undertones of fertility and reproduction (and fear of migrant fertility and reproduction) which Walters' term also carries and which reflect a long-standing concern of those who would control movement across national borders. Lonergan focuses on how policies she considers "domopolitical" construct and constrain the ways migrant women "reproduce" the "national home". The association of (racialized) family with nation, and the control of women's fertility (and its "purity") have long been linked with desires to defend national identity (see, among others, Yuval-Davis 1993). Domopolitics aiming to imagine a national "home" – however exclusive or inclusive access to that "home" might be – will always be domesticating, showing force not just towards "external" threats to safety, comfort, etc, but also to internal ones. Those who are deemed part of a family/home are expected to help one another out "simply because they belong" (Hill Collins 1998, 71); this simplicity of belonging is appealing and sustains the "More in Common" idea.

Here, Ghassan Hage's use of the concept of "domestication" is useful. Hage conceives domestication as a "colonial mode of instrumentalising, dominating, and exploiting the natural world, as well as differentiating oneself from it" (2016, 38). This encompasses the practices large and small through which humans (as individuals and socially) place themselves at the centre of importance, and organize life and its environs to their own advantage (Hage 2017; see also Bauman 1991). This might involve domestication of crops and livestock to produce food resources humans need or want; arranging a living room so that the light points a particular way and the temperature is pleasing; the colonization and exploitation of people and resources; or

44   RACIAL NATIONALISMS

the changing of conversations or focus so that some of these things can be more easily achieved. We might also think of it as making ourselves comfortable (Jones 2013).

In a striking analogy, Hage illustrates how domestication can be used to understand policies and practices like multiculturalism as means of taming the other, and on a spectrum with more obviously violent and silencing colonial processes such as slavery or extermination:

> Multiculturalism stands to assimilation in the way freerange chooks [Australian informal term for "chickens"] stand to battery [i.e. caged] hens. Free-range chooks are certainly ... freer than battery hens and living a healthier and happier life ... Nonetheless it should be remembered that neither process of farming chicken has the interest of the animal other as its final aim. (Hage 2016, 46; original insertions)

This imagery demonstrates how attempts to mitigate oppression, while they may improve some aspects of life, do not make a fundamental difference if they do not deal with the basic terms of the relation of power – the chickens may have a happier life, but they are still to be slaughtered. The analogy is with inclusion practices based on "tolerance", which may improve social relations on the surface, yet the powerful remain in charge with others able to exist only with their permission. Hage references how Muslims from the Global South are figured in ideas of threat, belonging and nationhood in white-dominated societies, in particular, settler colonial societies, and most specifically Australia. In discussing the "*état de siège*" experienced by white-majority countries in relation to migration from the majority world, Hage notes that anti-racist analyses tend to argue that while people may really feel threatened, the actual threat itself is fictional and "Western colonial societies 'really' have nothing to worry about" (2016, 45). He questions the completeness of such analysis, asking:

> why can't Islamophobia be a racist mode of *coming to terms* with a real threat, a threat to the colonial order, as opposed to the racist *manufacturing* of a nonexistent threat? (Hage 2016, 45; original emphasis)

Hage's implication is not that Muslim populations are the kind of threat imagined by racist Islamophobes (taking our daughters, etc.) but that their presence and/or demands for equality may indeed form a challenge to institutionalized white supremacy which may have to give way to more democratic or uncertain forms of society – and *this* is a real "threat". The reaction to this threat – violent and virulent Islamophobia – reimagines and distorts the threat and remains a racist *reaction*. Hage suggests that while the dismissal of the idea that global movements of people represent any change (or "threat") may be meant in a spirit of "welcome", it instead promotes an idea of powerlessness and benignity, removing agency from the people it is intended to "defend":

the task is no longer to say … "There is no threat here." Rather, we must say, "Yes, there is something threatening this increasingly toxic modern colonial order, and just as well!" Now, how are we to negotiate this something? (Hage 2016, 48)

How does this translate to an understanding of the violent incursions of visible white supremacy into political life? My argument is that there is indeed something to be reckoned with in terms of political differences. Women and racially minoritized people (including of course racially minoritized women) are increasingly taking on positions of power in British life. They are not always feminists or anti-racists of course, but many are – and they are taking up space that white patriarchy would otherwise expect to maintain. "More in Common" responses imagine that the killer's misogynist white supremacy is an aberration. This fails to recognize a more disturbing phenomenon; the pervasiveness of "polite" misogynist white supremacy in political and social life.

Are British values anti-racist feminist values?

For the last two decades, under governments of various parties, politicians have been trying to define "British values" as if these can be both inclusive and definitive. Currently, "fundamental" British values – defined as "democracy, rule of law, equality of opportunity, freedom of speech and the rights of all … to live free from persecution" (H.M. Government 2011, 34) – are expected to be taught in schools; public sector workers must report any suspicion people are "undermining" such values to counter-terrorism officers. Government has also stated that "intolerance of other cultures and gender inequality" is "contrary to British values" (H.M. Government 2011, 68).

There is plenty to critique within the British values agenda – that these values are characteristic of British behaviour, or that they are particular to Britain, for example. Yet it has much mileage in government. In December 2016, the Conservative government produced another report they had commissioned on "integration" (Casey 2016), which describes the UK as welcoming migrants – and yet suggests that new migration adds new pressures, and that political leaders have failed to address this because they are scared of being labelled racist. The report does not engage with how "new pressures" might relate to austerity, cuts to government services, or global politics and economics.

A well-publicized finding of the report was that abuse of women in Muslim communities was not being challenged. This was endorsed by, among others, Nigel Farage MEP (Farage 2016), who was suddenly, apparently, a feminist, as were right-wing newspapers which usually spend their time commenting on women's bodies (e.g. Press Association 2016). In an interview, the report's author discussed women unable to go out of their houses without their husbands' permission, claiming "if the women were white and living in Surrey, we'd be up in arms about it" (BBC News 2016). That same week, a feminist charity demonstrated that 936 women were killed in England and Wales between 2009 and 2015 in acts of femicide and domestic violence – that is, because they were women (Brennan 2016). Many of them were white, and they lived all over England and Wales. "We" – the general public – were not "up in arms"; it barely made a press mention. This is a classic example of the "misuse of feminism", where appeals for women's rights are prioritized only to make a point about the depravity of racially minoritized men (see Bhattacharyya 2008). In Walters' (2004) sense, the "national home" is taken for granted as safe except when threatened by racialized outsiders; the dangers to women within the "home" are irrelevant in this misogynistic white supremacist common sense except when mobilized to defend the border (see also Farris 2017).

We can see a related dynamic at play in the "More in Common" response to Cox's assassination. The campaign itself, and the association of the Jo Cox Foundation with campaign group Hope Not Hate, demonstrate a refusal of racism focused on the undomesticated extremism of those who overtly sign up to white supremacism; a refusal which is of course essential. However, this does not engage with how racism, like sexism, bathes all aspects of the culture in which we live, and fails to confront "the role of racialized nationalism in the definition of the populist political community" discussed in Ben Pitcher's contribution to this special issue. It similarly ignores the underlying misogyny of the attack.

A year on from Cox's death, her husband Brendan published a biography of her, predominantly a story of devastating private grief, yet also positioned as a political intervention in memory of his wife (Cox 2017). The book characterizes Cox as a wife and mother with local, domestic roots. This aspect of her life was undoubtedly the most important and devastating loss for those close to the person, Jo Cox. And yet the significance of her murder as a national event cannot end there.

Brendan's memoir describes Cox as "loving", "warm", "shining", "strong", ambitious – while "small", "feisty", and with a "distinctive" Yorkshire accent. Something seems to be lost of Cox as a real woman as Brendan writes about her. The moments when she comes alive as a more complex character are in extracts he uses from her diaries – for example, she describes herself as having a "sarcastic nature" (63) and asks whether she should temper her sarcasm to fit in. This aspect of her "nature" is never otherwise mentioned by Brendan; she is more likely to be "plain-speaking" (86) "sunny and optimistic" (120), with "an easy smile and a devilish sense of fun" (212). Gender norms are constantly reinforced in the telling of this life: in the image of Cox's "essence" and "nature" constantly expressed; in the way Brendan positions himself as doing equal parenting while describing the ways he does not (e.g. 219–220); in his exploits such as grabbing a big pole to smash the ice around their houseboat and save them; in him proposing to her without discussing it in advance; announcing her pregnancy without her permission; in how remarkable it seemingly is when she carries his bag when he is injured. These gendered tropes of infantilized womanhood re-situate someone described elsewhere as "an extremely talented MP ... a proud Labour feminist" (Labour Party, n.d.). Her husband of course mourns the loss of his wife and the way he knew her, but in doing so in this public way, in a book positioned as a political intervention, this domestication of her memory risks missing the importance of her role as a political force in her own right.

Similarly, the treatment of race in the book is far from a critically-informed anti-racist standpoint – from the language used to discuss racialized voting patterns (261); to the depiction of Cox's empathy and strength through an image of her "holding hands" with Darfuri rape victims reproducing white saviour tropes (119); to Brendan professing a belief that "fundamental rights and principles of equality ... were sacrosanct in America" (175) until the election of Trump, suggesting a shocking lack of understanding of race politics and history for a former Prime Ministerial advisor. This superficial anti-racism is important because it gestures to a hostility to racism without deeply engaging, recognizing, and reckoning with pervasive white supremacy. To express political resistance to Donald Trump's presidency on the basis of his "naked bigotry" (175) as a contrast to timeless values of the USA, rather than as a step backwards in the direction of the founding of the USA as a state built (with the British) on extermination and enslavement of peoples, is to miss important context for the political moment. Trump's appeal is his promise to re-instate a more forthright and unapologetic misogynist white supremacy; but it is to re-instate it, not to invent it. Further, ignoring the realities of ongoing white supremacism hampers the possibility of solidarity across its power imbalances; it domesticates the reality of political division in an attempt at a bland consensus centrism which accommodates rather than threatens the misogynist white supremacist order.

This erasure, or domestication, of power struggles is also visible in public-focused More in Common interventions. On the first anniversary of the murder, people around the UK gathered for "The Great Get Together", street parties and picnics to assert the "More in Common" idea through shared food and conviviality, "love" in defiance of "hatred" (notwithstanding the emphasis on eating and drinking as what "we have in common" during the Ramadan fast might have been awkward). This was a pure expression of domopolitics. Interrogation of political differences and power were obscured in favour of a populist diversity drawing intransigently on the racialized nation state as its base (see Pitcher, this issue). Let's watch a video of a series of celebrities publicizing this event:

The video opens with a drawing of Jo Cox and the quotation: "We are far more united and have far more in common than that which divides us."

Patriotic orchestral music starts playing,[1] a pink gingham frame appears with the words "The Great Get Together" in the top left-hand corner, and a series of celebrities (most of whom at some point have been described as "national treasures"), apparently sitting in their living rooms, appear one by one and speak to camera:

Helen Mirren:[2]	So what does unite us as a country?
Ed Sheeran:[3]	Fish and chips. Yeah.
Andy Murray:[4]	Everyone loves a bit of 007 don't they?
Nadiya Hussain: [5]	Cake. Correct me if I'm wrong!
Andy Murray:	Sean Connery's the best one for sure.
Jamie Carragher:[6]	Sport is what unites our great country.
Stephen Fry:[7]	Tea and biscuits.
Minnie Driver:[8]	Tea and hot cross buns.
Bill Nighy:[9]	Toast … Unless it's spread with Marmite.
Helen Mirren:	We love our pubs. We LOVE our pubs.
Stephen Fry:	I do find the British generally speaking cheerful.
Andrew Marr:[10]	Stroppy.
Claire Balding:[11]	Stoical and brave.
June Sarpong:[12]	A society where difference is valued.
Bill Nighy:	A genuine concern for other people's welfare.
Nadiya Hussain:	No matter who we are, where we're from.
Girl at street party (member of the public):	We're all one race, and that's human.
David Haye:[13]	Moaning, it's such a British thing.
Helen Mirren:	I think our bloody-mindedness, as well.
David Haye:	The weather. It's either too hot, too cold, too wet, too sticky.
Adil Ray:[14]	I would say it's openness.
Martin Sheen:[15]	A sense of outrage at any injustice.
Andrew Marr:	Our sense of humour.
Claire Balding:[16]	Morecambe and Wise or Miranda Hart or French and Saunders, or John Cleese doing a silly walk.
Helen Mirren:[17]	We all love Dame Judi Dench.
Ed Sheeran:	I think the things that unite us as a country are the things that are meant to tear us apart, but they actually make us stronger.
Claire Balding:	What else?
Woman at street party (member of the public):	L.O.V.E. Love [laughs].
Helen Mirren:	What do you think unites us a country?
Ed Sheeran:	Share this video and tell us what you think.

The screen is filled completely with pink gingham. Then the logo "The Great Get Together", underneath "Inspired by Jo Cox". Finally, on a black screen, white writing with a red swirl passing across it (reminiscent of the St George's cross of the English flag): "Please share #moreincommon greatgettogether.org". (Author's transcript of Great Get Together 2017)

In amongst the banal patriotism and suggestion that nationalism (expressed through love of elderly actors and jovial disagreement about sandwich spreads) is a common sense accepted by all – and has something to do with combatting hatred – the closest we get to dissent is actor Martin Sheen's claim that antagonism to injustice is "what unites us as a nation". The setting of this celebration is the nostalgic, feminized, domestic iconography of pink gingham picnic blankets. Women and racially minoritized people are present and speak directly – but without outrage from anyone about the assassination or any other injustice. Such a challenge would rip apart the comfort of the picnic blanket; it might represent the direct "threat" to misogynist white supremacism which is here entirely domesticated.

This critique of the Great Get Together is not meant to malign the good intentions of those involved. Considering a widower's memoir of his assassinated partner is not intended to intrude on or minimize grief. But it seems important to highlight how interventions positioned against anti-democratic, white supremacist violence, can reproduce the everyday, domesticating and domesticated common-sense of misogynist white supremacy. That this turns out to be the case should not be surprising; we live in a society premised on misogynist white supremacy. It is the basis of the organization of society and the distribution of power and authority. This is also why it is unsurprising that when liberation struggles of marginalized groups result in women and racially minoritized people beginning to gain positions of authority, violent outbreaks of undomesticated misogynist white supremacy arise, no matter how far those liberation struggles have been domesticated to prevent underlying power relations being addressed.

Breaking point: one deranged individual?

The day that Jo Cox was brutally murdered, Nigel Farage (Member of the European Parliament, prominent Leave.EU campaigner and leader of the UK Independence Party) revealed a campaign poster claiming the UK was at "Breaking Point" because of immigration (mixed up with refugees), and that a vote to leave the EU would solve that (see also articles by Abbas and by Pitcher in this special issue). The man who murdered Cox later in the day shouted "Britain First", the name of a far-right organization which has aligned itself with Farage's party and policies (Cusick 2015). When, among the outpourings of solidarity, sorrow and defiance in the wake of Cox's murder, the parallels between some Leave campaign rhetoric and the murderer's motivations were pointed out, Farage responded that the murder was down to "one deranged, dangerous individual" (M. Smith 2016), dismissing any consideration that the tenor of political debate may have contributed to a climate of hate and fear. The day after the EU referendum – a week after the shooting – Farage said the Leave campaign had won "without a single bullet being fired" (Saul 2016).

50 RACIAL NATIONALISMS

In December 2016, two weeks after the conviction of Cox's murderer, another man was convicted for abuse of a female MP, Luciana Berger. Berger was not physically attacked, but she was subject to a concerted campaign of anti-semitic, misogynist abuse on social media and in her private life, including 2,500 messages a day at some points from organized neo-Nazis (P. Smith 2016). In November 2017, two members of a banned white supremacist group, National Action, were charged in connection with a plot to kill another female Labour MP, Rosie Cooper, to which one man pleaded guilty to preparing an act of terrorism by buying a machete for the purpose of the planned murder (Dearden 2017; BBC News 2018b). In January 2018, a far-right group, the White Pendragons, attempted to make a "citizen's arrest" of Labour London Mayor, Sadiq Khan, for "subverting our English constitution", apparently on the basis of his (Muslim) religion, as he made a speech on gender equality to the Fabian Society (Johnston 2018). They also "brought a homemade gallows with them to London" (TellMAMA 2018). That same month, a man was convicted for murder and attempted murder after driving a vehicle into worshippers at the Finsbury Park mosque in June 2017, stating in court that his initial intention had been to murder Labour Party leader, Jeremy Corbyn, at a march that day, adding that if Sadiq Khan had also been present "It would have been like winning the lottery" (BBC News 2018a). An increase in verbal and physical attacks on MPs was documented after the 2017 election (Wheeler and Carter 2017), with evidence that women and racially minoritized candidates face the worst abuse (BBC News 2017). Diane Abbott MP, the Shadow Home Secretary at the 2017 general election and the UK's first black woman MP, faced the very worst of it – 45 per cent of all 25,688 abusive tweets to female MPs during the election campaign were personally directed at Abbott (Dhrodia 2017).

These attacks or planned attacks were on specific individuals. They were not targeted as "ordinary people". Nor were they attacked precisely because of who they are personally. They were symbolic for the attackers, as leftists, liberals, racially minoritized people and their supporters, Jewish and Muslim people and their supporters, migrants and supporters of migrant rights, and women and feminist men. Arguing that there is "More in Common" between Jo Cox (or Diane Abbott), and the people who hate Jo Cox (or Diane Abbott) – as individuals, and for the politics and values they represent – misunderstands the problem. It turns the problem into a cosy, domopolitical question of "getting along" in the home, rather than an oppositional political struggle attempting to silence a (feminist and/or racially minoritized) "other".

The political and media response to the assassination of Jo Cox has domesticated it as if it was an attack on a member of the public, emphasizing the implications for her family. The images of Cox in her wedding dress used on the front pages of national newspapers including *The Daily Mirror, The*

Guardian, and the *i* at the close of her murderer's trial were clearly intended to memorialize the joy in her life rather than remembering her solely for her terrible death. Yet they also put her role as wife and mother, rather than as political representative, to the fore, as did newspaper cover stories on the day after her death. In *The Sun*:

> MURDERED IN COLD BLOOD
> Husband's moving tribute as MP shot 3 times and knifed 7 times by crazed loner
> MY JO
> The husband of MP Jo Cox wrote a poignant tribute to his wife less than an hour after she was murdered by a crazed loner yesterday. Heartbroken Brendan Cox also tweeted a photo of her by the River Thames, where the couple lived on a boat with their two young children. Jo, 41, was shot three times and stabbed seven times in her West Yorks constituency yesterday afternoon. (Sims 2016).

This was accompanied by images of Cox by their boat ("Home ... photo tweeted by husband Brendan showing Jo by Thames") and of the couple at their wedding ("HUSBAND Brendan & Jo on wedding day") and a photo of the murderer ("'KILLER' Loner Thomas Mair"). And in *The Daily Mail:*

> Devoted mother of two. Dedicated public servant. MP Jo Cox was a remarkable woman. Yesterday she was brutally murdered by a loner with a history of mental illness.
> WHAT A TRAGIC WASTE
> The husband of an MP allegedly murdered by a troubled loner last night called on Britain to unite and "fight against the hatred that killed her" ... The rising Labour star and dedicated MP died from catastrophic injuries ... Witnesses saw the gunman shout "put Britain first" as he kicked, stabbed and then shot the slightly-built 5ft mother-of-two .... (Greenwood, Brooke, and Dolan 2016)

These front pages of the two highest circulation UK newspapers focused on Cox's relationship to her husband and children as the most pressing aspect of her murder, not her democratic role. Though a "rising Labour star" in the *Mail*, *The Sun* does not even acknowledge which party Cox represented; both focus on the brutality of the attack, by a "crazed" or "troubled" "loner", and on the consequences for Brendan (and their children). The description of Cox's physique in the *Mail* ("the slightly-built 5ft mother-of-two") is in line with Brendan's victim statement to the court regarding the murderer:

> ... his only way of finding meaning was to attack a defenceless woman .... (Cox 2017, 212)

Cox, in these presentations, is a vulnerable feminine victim of random violence, rather than a political target. The focus on her family's grief as the key site of violence continued throughout reporting and memorialization of this political assassination (e.g. Griffiths 2017; ITV 2017; Falvey 2018).

Though the concern for Cox's family is important, to make this the focus of national grief is to de-politicise this political assassination – or rather, it is to re-politicise it in a particularly gendered and domesticated way. Focusing on the tragedy of a young woman of potential being murdered (rather than a political figure) is a way of domesticating the narrative. It reduces Cox to only what the attacker thought she should be – a wife and mother – and reminds us that in broader British society, the domestic or family role is still seen as fundamental to the identity of a woman, no matter what her political or other engagements. In Hage's terms, it minimizes the "threat" that Cox and the feminist, anti-racist, pro-migrant internationalism she was seen to stand for posed to the white supremacism which her killer sought to defend.[18] By recloaking her as a first and foremost a harmless, "defenceless woman", it fails to say that "Yes, there is something threatening this increasingly toxic modern colonial [and patriarchal] order, and just as well" – an order that the killer wished to defend with his crime (Hage 2016, 48). Instead, her murder is taken out of this context and re-homed within the domestic, but as a meaningless attack on the idealized home represented by a (white) wife and mother.

Resisting the domestication of misogynist white supremacy

Jo Cox's murder was named as a political assassination by her family and political colleagues, and tried as such in the criminal justice system. However, the loudest voices memorializing her have identified the target of the assassination as the idea that "we have more in common than that which divides us". Their response has been to demonstrate such commonality through a re-articulation of fundamental British identity as embodied in shared tea and cake, pubs and celebrities. This sits alongside re-assertion of "British values" as being associated with equality, particularly gender equality, and against discrimination. This presents, as I have demonstrated drawing on Walters' "domopolitics" and Hage's "domestication", a double sense of the domestic, where the nation is imagined as a cosy home in which food, drink and entertainment unite the (national) family, and a national home in which shared values embrace and are embraced by all.

In Malcolm James' paper in this special issue, he argues for acts of care as a means of confronting cruelty; but here I have shown that if events like the Great Get Together are imagined as acts of care, they still fail to confront the cruelty of misogynist white supremacy, and indeed reproduce some of its everyday forms (see also Sirriyeh 2018). Actions centred on the performance of "shared values" of care depend on the idea that Cox's assassination was an anomaly, the work of "one deranged individual", an outsider to the "More in Common" consensus – and to the national home. As I have shown, though his violent misogynist white supremacy was extreme and unregulated, it was not out of step with wider patterns. We can see this in the way everyday untimely deaths of women – whether confronting the violence of international borders at sea, or at the hands of their immediate family in their own homes – are rarely of political interest except as a tool to pathologise racialized others. It is visible too in the pattern of targeted verbal and physical attacks on prominent feminists and anti-racists, and particularly the virulence of attacks on racially minoritized women in the public eye.

So what is the alternative to "More in Common" and its domestication of political conflict? It is to resist the simplification and the pull towards comforting narratives. What is needed is a refusal to repair existing systems of misogynist white supremacist power and knowledge. Cox's murderer *did* identify an anomaly: that the presence of Cox and others like her *do* represent a threat, however latent, to misogynist white supremacy – and "just as well!" as Hage would say. However, the threat she – we – represent has been largely domesticated, neutered, by the reincorporation of liberation struggles into existing structures – for example, through "diversity agendas" over-taking equity demands (Ahmed 2012), through neoliberal market prerogatives dominating free movement politics (Pitcher, this issue), or through the appropriation of feminist agendas for the purpose of racialized border control (Bhattacharyya 2008; Farris 2017). Feminist anti-racist politics is not (yet) a hegemonic common-sense (Ahmed 2008). It is rather an internal contradiction in the system of misogynist white supremacy.

A proper response to Cox's assassination must place it in social, political and historical context. It must recognize – at the very least – that this took place at a moment of enormous political cleavage signalled by the Brexit campaign, and forms part of a pattern of "backlash" against the increasing prominence of women, racialized minorities, and their supporters, in public life. The answer to that is not to imagine a shared, easy – but inevitably illusory and unsustainable – centrist consensus, where all will feel "at home" in domestic bliss, but to identify the connections between the unruly extremes of misogynist white supremacism and its everyday forms found in politics (Dhrodia 2017; Wheeler and Carter 2017), institutions (Puwar 2004) and the home (Barrett and McIntosh [1982] 2014; Brennan 2016; Lonergan 2018). Though the moment requires a much broader societal movement, the Jo Cox Women in Leadership programme (Labour Party, n.d.), as an explicitly feminist and (less explicitly) anti-racist action supporting more women (including racially minoritized women) into positions of power, is a far more appropriate response to Cox's assassination than community picnics. Acknowledging and confronting the political differences and power imbalances which underpin British society is the only way to come to terms with Jo Cox's assassination in a way which does justice to its significance for political life.

Notes

1. Handel's *Zadok the Priest,* written for the coronation of King George II in 1727 and played at the coronation of British monarchs ever since.
2. Actor.
3. Musician.
4. Tennis player.
5. TV chef.
6. Footballer.
7. Actor.
8. Actor.
9. Actor.
10. Journalist.
11. TV presenter.
12. TV presenter.
13. Boxer.
14. Actor.
15. Actor.
16. All British comedians.
17. Actor.
18. The purity of Cox's anti-racism or other politics are not the point; her position of relative power as a woman, and her statements on Syrian refugees, multiculturalism, feminism and Brexit meant she posed enough of a threat for her murderer to fear.

Acknowledgements

Thank you to the other participants and the organizers of the *Racism, Anti-Racism and Managing the Crisis* symposium at the University of Manchester in December 2016 at which a version of this paper was first presented. Thank you for background detail to Hrishikesh and Rick Jones, Naaz Rashid, and Anne Malcolm and her parents.

Disclosure statement

No potential conflict of interest was reported by the author.

ORCID

Hannah Jones ⓘ http://orcid.org/0000-0002-2508-0284

References

Ahmed, S. 2008. "Liberal Multiculturalism is the Hegemony – It's an Empirical Fact – A Response to Slavoj Žižek." *Dark Matter*, February 19. http://www.darkmatter101.org/site/2008/02/19/%E2%80%98liberal-multiculturalism-is-the-hegemony-%E2%80%93-its-an-empirical-fact%E2%80%99-a-response-to-slavoj-zizek/.
Ahmed, S. 2012. *On Being Included: Racism and Diversity in Institutional Life.* Durham, NC: Duke University Press.

Barrett, M., and M. McIntosh. [1982] 2014. *The Anti-social Family*. Reprint, London: Verso.

Bauman, Z. 1991. *Modernity and the Holocaust*. London: Polity.

BBC News. 2016. "Segregation at 'Worrying Levels' in Parts of Britain, Dame Louise Casey Warns." *BBC News*, December 5. http://www.bbc.co.uk/news/uk-38200989.

BBC News. 2017. "Jewish and Muslim Women MPs 'Face Most Abuse'." *BBC News*, March 21. http://www.bbc.co.uk/news/uk-politics-39339487.

BBC News. 2018a. "Darren Osborne Guilty of Finsbury Park Mosque Murder." *BBC News*, February 1. http://www.bbc.co.uk/news/uk-42910051.

BBC News. 2018b. "National Action: Men Jailed for Being Members of Banned Neo-Nazi Group." *BBC News*, July 18. https://www.bbc.co.uk/news/uk-politics-44873178.

Bhattacharyya, G. 2008. *Dangerous Brown Men: Exploiting Sex, Violence and Feminism in the "War on Terror"*. London: Zed Books.

Brennan, D. 2016. *Femicide Census: Profiles of Women Killed by Men, Redefining an Isolated Incident*. London: Women's Aid and nia.

Casey, L. 2016. *The Casey Review: A Review into Opportunity and Integration*. London: DCLG.

Cobain, I., N. Parveen, and M. Taylor. 2016. "The Slow-burning Hatred that Led Thomas Mair to Murder Jo Cox." *The Guardian*, November 23. https://www.theguardian.com/uk-news/2016/nov/23/thomas-mair-slow-burning-hatred-led-to-jo-cox-murder.

Cobain, I., and M. Taylor. 2016. "Far-right Terrorist Thomas Mair Jailed for Life for Jo Cox Murder." *The Guardian*, November 23. https://www.theguardian.com/uk-news/2016/nov/23/thomas-mair-found-guilty-of-jo-cox-murder.

Cox, B. 2017. *Jo Cox: More in Common*. London: Two Roads.

Cusick, J. 2015. "Vote UKIP, Says Far-right Group Britain First." *The Independent*, March 22. http://www.independent.co.uk/news/uk/politics/vote-ukip-say-far-right-group-britain-first-10126389.html.

Dearden, L. 2017. "National Action: Alleged Neo-Nazi 'Who Bought Machete to Murder Labour MP Rosie Cooper' Appears in Court." *The Independent*, November 3. https://www.independent.co.uk/news/uk/crime/national-action-trial-latest-updates-neo-nazi-machet-rosie-cooper-labour-mp-murder-plot-court-a8036166.html.

Dhrodia, A. 2017. "We Tracked 25,688 Abusive Tweets Sent to Women MPs – Half were Directed at Diane Abbott." *New Statesman*, September 5. https://www.newstatesman.com/2017/09/we-tracked-25688-abusive-tweets-sent-women-mps-half-were-directed-diane-abbott.

Du Bois, W. E. B. [1920] 1969. *Darkwater: Voices From Within the Veil*. New York: AMS Press.

Falvey, D. 2018. "Theresa May Delivers Emotional Heartfelt Message to Jo Cox's Children About 'Mummy'." *Sunday Express*, January 18. https://www.express.co.uk/news/uk/906339/jo-cox-minister-for-loneliness-theresa-may-tracey-crouch-labour-mp-murder.

Farage, N. 2016. Twitter Post, December 5, 9:50 AM. Accessed March 23, 2018. https://twitter.com/Nigel_Farage/status/805710969603293184.

Farris, S. R. 2017. *In the Name of Women's Rights: The Rise of Femonationalism*. Durham, NC: Duke University Press.

Freedman, D. 2017. "Media Power and the Framing of the Charlie Hebdo Attacks." In *After Charlie Hebdo: Terror, Racism and Free Speech*, edited by G. Titley, D. Freedman, G. Khiabany, and A. Mondon, 209–222. London: Zed Books.

Gallagher, C., and F. Winddance Twine. 2017. "From Wave to Tsunami: The Growth of Third Wave Whiteness." *Ethnic and Racial Studies* 40 (9): 1598–1603.

Great Get Together. 2017. "The Great Get Together Aims to Unite Britain for Jo Cox." Video. Accessed February 8, 2018. https://www.youtube.com/watch?v=pgQf8JMX3_0.

Greenwood, C., C. Brooke, and A. Dolan. 2016. "What a Tragic Waste." *The Daily Mail*, June 17.

Griffiths, B. 2017. "WIDOWER TELLS ALL Jo Cox's Husband Brendan Reveals Taking Kids to See Murdered Wife's Body 'was the Hardest Decision of His Life'." *The Sun*, June 4. https://www.thesun.co.uk/news/3718639/jo-coxs-husband-brendan-reveals-taking-kids-to-see-murdered-wifes-body-was-the-hardest-decision-of-his-life/.

H.M. Government. 2011. *Prevent Strategy*. London: TSO.

Hage, G. 2016. "État de Siege: A Dying Domesticated Colonialism?" *American Ethnologist* 43 (1): 38–49.

Hage, G. 2017. *Is Racism an Environmental Threat?* London: Wiley.

Hansard. 2015. HC Deb 3 June 2015, vol 596, cols 674-5.

Hill Collins, P. 1998. "It's All in the Family: Intersections of Gender, Race and Nation." *Hypatia* 13 (3): 62–82.

ITV. 2017. "Jo Cox's Children Set to Unveil Coat of Arms Dedicated to Mum." *ITV News*, June 24. http://www.itv.com/news/2017-06-24/jo-coxs-children-unveil-coat-of-arms-dedicated-to-mum/.

Jo Cox Foundation. n.d. "The Issues." Accessed March 21, 2018. https://www.jocoxfoundation.org/the-issues/.

Johnston, C. 2018. "Sadiq Khan Speech Disrupted by Brexit and Trump Supporters." *The Guardian*, January 13. https://www.theguardian.com/politics/2018/jan/13/sadiq-khan-speech-disrupted-by-protesters-backing-brexit-and-trump-white-pendragons.

Jones, H. 2013. *Negotiating Cohesion, Inequality and Change: Uncomfortable Positions in Local Government*. Bristol: Policy Press.

Jones, H., Y. Gunaratnam, G. Bhattacharyya, W. Davies, S. Dhaliwal, K. Forkert, E. Jackson, and R. Saltus. 2017. *Go Home? The Politics of Immigration Controversies*. Manchester: MUP.

Labour Party. n.d. "The Jo Cox Women in Leadership Programme." Accessed November 15, 2018. https://labour.org.uk/members/jo-cox-women-leadership/.

Lonergan, G. 2018. "Reproducing the 'National Home': Gendering Domopolitics." *Citizenship Studies* 22 (1): 1–18.

Press Association. 2016. "Misogyny and Patriarchy Widening Inequality, Says Integration Report Author." *Daily Mail*, December 6. http://www.dailymail.co.uk/wires/pa/article-3999968/Pupils-taught-British-values-help-bind-communities-review-says.html#ixzz5AfOfl8jK.

Puwar, N. 2004. *Space Invaders: Race, Gender and Bodies out of Place*. London: Berg.

Saul, H. 2016. "Brexit: Nigel Farage Branded 'Shameful' for Claiming Victory 'Without a Single Bullet Being Fired'." *The Independent*, June 24. https://www.independent.co.uk/news/people/eu-referendum-nigel-farage-branded-shameful-for-claiming-victory-without-a-single-bullet-being-fired-a7099211.html.

Sims, P. 2016. "Murdered in Cold Blood." *The Sun*, June 17.

Sirriyeh, A. 2018. *The Politics of Compassion: Immigration and Asylum Policy*. Bristol: BUP.

Smith, P. 2016. "Jewish MP Feared For Her Safety After Receiving 2,500 Abusive Messages A Day." *BuzzFeed News*, December 5. https://www.buzzfeed.com/patricksmith/jewish-mp-feared-for-her-safety-after-receiving-2500-abusive?utm_term=.moxBv57P7#.clxvn6qwq.

Smith, M. 2016. "Nigel Farage Claims 'ALL of the Remain Camp' are 'Using' Jo Cox's Death for Their Political Advantage." *The Mirror*, June 20. https://www.mirror.co.uk/news/uk-news/nigel-farage-claims-all-remain-8236531.

TellMAMA. 2018. "Who are the White Pendragons?" January 15. http://tellmamauk.org/who-are-the-white-pendragons/.

Walters, W. 2004. "Secure Borders, Safe Haven, Domopolitics." *Citizenship Studies* 8 (3): 237–260.

Wekker, G. 2016. *White Innocence: Paradoxes of Colonialism and Race*. Durham, NC: Duke University Press.

Wheeler, B., and A. Carter. 2017. "MPs Tell of Death Threats and Abuse at 2017 Election." *BBC News*, September 18. http://www.bbc.co.uk/news/uk-politics-41237836.

Yuval-Davis, N. 1993. "Gender and Nation." *Ethnic and Racial Studies* 16 (4): 621–632.

Yuval-Davis, N., F. Anthias, and E. Kofman. 2005. "Secure Borders and Safe Haven and the Gendered Politics of Belonging: Beyond Social Cohesion." *Ethnic and Racial Studies* 28 (3): 513–535.

ⓐ OPEN ACCESS

Conflating the Muslim refugee and the terror suspect: responses to the Syrian refugee "crisis" in Brexit Britain

Madeline-Sophie Abbas ⓘ

ABSTRACT
The Syrian refugee "crisis" has prompted contradictory responses of securitization of European borders on the one hand, and grassroots compassion on the other, that posit a universal conception of the human deserving of equal rights to safety irrespective of racial or religious difference. However, in the aftermath of the 2015 and 2016 Paris terror attacks there has been a backlash against refugees amid fears of Islamist terrorists exploiting refugee channels to enter Europe, as well as an upsurge in a populist nationalism framing Brexit and anti-Muslim hostility following recent UK terror attacks. I argue that the convergence of the "Muslim refugee" and the "terror suspect" as threatening mobilizes a racialized biopolitics present in intersecting counter-terrorism and asylum regimes that prioritise security concerns above human rights. I advance the Concentrationary Gothic as a framework for understanding continuities in logics of racial terror framing the "Muslim question" within the Syrian refugee "crisis."

Introduction: racial terror and the refugee

The introduction of the 1951 Refugee Convention associated with the "Age of Rights" following the horrors of World War Two recognised human rights as foundational issues whereby, at least officially, refugees' struggles for freedom should be accommodated within democratic societies (Marfleet 2012, 69). A new epoch had emerged which Rousset (1946) coined the "concentrationary universe" to capture the terrors of totalitarian rule in which "everything is possible" (141). For Rousset, the concentrationary universe characterized the extension of an existing political system based on terror in which its victims are vanquished of social humanity but which was not confined within it (Pollock and Silverman 2011, 18). The concentration

---

This is an Open Access article distributed under the terms of the Creative Commons Attribution License (http://creativecommons.org/licenses/by/4.0/), which permits unrestricted use, distribution, and reproduction in any medium, provided the original work is properly cited.

camp is emblematic of this universe but it also references the society of which the camp is an instrument (Pollock and Silverman 2014, 3). The concentrationary provides a "historical and conceptual tool" (Pollock and Silverman 2011, 3) that is useful for drawing (dis)continuities between systems of terror and how they are racialized. Explicitly realized in Nazi Germany, the concentration camp has precedents within colonial contexts and subsequent manifestations that require that we be vigilant to signs of its recurrence (Arendt 1979; Gilroy 2000; Pollock and Silverman 2011, 13). The concentrationary is coextensive with the politico-juridical development of the normalization of the state of exception (Agamben 1998; Mbembe 2003; Razack 2008).

In my advancement of the Concentrationary Gothic as a framework for examining the mechanisms of racial terror (Abbas 2013, forthcoming), I argue that the concentrationary as a prism for understanding the operation of racial terror in states of exception and other structures of domination (Pollock and Silverman 2011, 14, 2014, 2–3) works in conjunction with practices of Gothicisation in support of white dominance (Abbas 2013). I follow Mighall's (1999, xviii) historical approach to the Gothic as representing the culture stigmatized as "uncivilized, unprogressive or 'barbaric.'" As explored elsewhere, "this representation shifts depending on the current socio-political and cultural attitudes so that at certain historical junctures, people (as well as institutions and places) are 'Gothicized,'" (Abbas 2013, unpaginated) that is; "they have the Gothic thrust upon them" (Mighall 1999: xxv) and by contrast, the "civilized self" (Punter and Byron 2003, 5) is defined.

Whilst acknowledging my debt to Said's (2003) *Orientalism* for understanding how European constructions of the colonized as inferior served purposes of domination, I argue that "racial gothic" (Malchow 1996, 2) provides a more useful vocabulary for exploring racial and cultural difference as unnatural. This is because it draws from parallel discourses of the human sciences, anthropology, and biology to articulate how categories of sub/human are constructed and contested and are tied to registers of hygiene and circuits of affective repulsion that are cogently expressed through Gothic tropes of the monster or monstrous, hauntings and the spectral, and abjected states. Attention to Gothic discourses alerts us to how human rights are subsumed within systems of racial terror that are significant for understanding the "Muslim question" and its articulation within a historical trajectory of terror against racialized others (Abbas 2013, forthcoming).

The Concentrationary Gothic foregrounds how Gothic discourses are used to support racialized biopolitics involved in practices of governance and dominance that comprise nation construction and exclusion, racial profiling and screening/surveillance practices, spatial control, restrictions to freedom of speech and political engagement, and production of internal divisions within the oppressed group. Elsewhere I applied the Concentrationary Gothic framework to examine the terrors of counter-terrorism measures experienced by British Muslims within the "war on terror" context (Abbas

60

2013, forthcoming). Here I use the Concentrationary Gothic framework to show how similar mechanisms have been deployed during the Syrian refugee "crisis." I approach the UK government's Syrian Vulnerable Persons Relocation Scheme (VPRS) as an example of racial biopolitics that is part of a wider shift in focus from human rights to security in the treatment of asylum seekers (Huysmans 1995; Weber and Bowling 2004).

The article also examines two case studies which provide insight of how the Brexit context shapes articulations of the Syrian refugee through two Gothic discourses: firstly, "reverse colonisation," that expresses terrors of the purportedly "civilised' world being invaded by 'primitive forces'" (Arata 1990, 623; also Brantlinger 1988, 229) through analysis of the *Breaking Point* poster (see Pitcher this issue) used during the EU referendum campaign. The Gothic has persistently put to work anxieties about national identity as Schmitt (1997, 3) writes, whereby "the threat of invasion from without produces Englishness from within," thus invoking a virulent reassertion of Englishness. The poster draws on fears of the English being displaced so that "England itself becomes an alien nation" (Schmitt 1997, 3).

Secondly, the "discourse of degeneration" (Byron 2000, 132) through my advancement of the phantom "man-child" as a recent iteration of the deceitful Arab that draws together anxieties of the refugee violating Britain's hospitality and the Islamist terrorist who transgresses Britain's borders to enact atrocities against her inhabitants. I refer to the Home Office's commitment to resettling "vulnerable" children from the Calais camp known as the "Jungle" following its dissolution in October 2016 as part of the Dublin III agreement included in the Immigration Act 2016 which recognizes the human rights of refugee children with close family in the UK to be reunited. Vociferous debates accompanying this move around determining the ages of child refugees to be resettled provides another important instance of the operation of the human rights-security nexus and ways in which categories of the "human" and what is "humane" are contested. The discourse of degeneration present in fin de siècle Gothic texts is concerned with defining the contours of a culture "in crisis." It provides a counterpoint to scientific rigour and certainty by articulating fears of the "dissolution of the nation, of society, of the human subject itself" (Byron 2000, 133) and by contrast, the desire to identify and contain what is "unfixed, transgressive, other and threatening" (Byron 2000, 133) by demanding there "*be* a boundary" (Glover 1996, 71, original italics). Here, the "man-child" troubles attempts to classify and order bodies (Hurley 1996; Wagner 2012) and secure national borders by exposing the limits of science for determining the ages of asylum seekers and status as il/legitimate.

Context: Brexit Britain

Political mobilization of a populist rhetoric vilifying immigration repeatedly used by Brexiters during the EU referendum campaign in Britain emboldened the enactment of white nationalist sentiments (Mandaville 2017) previously contained beneath a veneer of acceptance towards Britain's racial minorities. Brexit raises particular questions concerning the relationship between Britain and Europe where the "Muslim question" is a significant political pawn, both in terms of refashioning British identity according to what Hage (1998) terms a "white nation fantasy," and implementing increasingly exclusionary border controls. Bordering has been central to Brexit with leave supporters expressing desire to "take back control" of Britain's borders. The argument runs that Britain could regain its powers as an autonomous sovereignty and avoid the responsibilities of membership to a global community.

Issues surrounding British identity and perceived failure of multiculturalism have often coalesced around the "Muslim question." Muslim communities are charged with bearing social ills of threats to national security and identity through self-segregation or "parallel lives" (Cantle 2001) post the 2001 disturbances in the north of England. More recently, Muslims have been accused of harbouring "regressive attitudes" (Casey Review 2016, 128). This articulation illustrates intersections of Gothic and racial discourses by associating Muslims with retrograde religious practices deemed incompatible with "modern Britain."

Politicization of demands for integration of which the Muslim is currently presented as the most troubling interloper, is reflected in racially charged public and policy debates which have taken on a violent impetus. The killing of MP Jo Cox (see Jones this issue), a passionate campaigner for refugees who was also working on a report with Tell MAMA on the rise of Islamophobia and aggressive nationalism (*Independent,* 20 June, 2016), illustrates the dangers of exclusionary border tactics when taken to their perverse limits. Her killer, Thomas Mair, had kept newspaper printings of her pro-remain position and support for refugees (Tell MAMA 2017, 13) and allegedly shouted "Britain First" during the attack – a far right organization which campaigns against multiculturalism and perceived "Islamisation" of Britain. As observed by TUC (2016) in their action plan for tackling increased racism and xenophobia following the 23 June 2016 referendum result, the campaign was characterized "by highly divisive rhetoric and sensationalist appeals to racial and national sentiment," that by conflating issues of immigration, the so-called "refugee crisis" in Europe and Islamic terrorism, encouraged resentment towards new and settled minority ethnic groups, and Muslims in particular.

Contemporary examinations of racial politics require paying attention to the particular ways in which Muslims are positioned as threatening bodies, both within the nation's borders and transnationally through a chain of signification which draws together anxieties concerning the immigrant, the refugee, and the terror suspect (Weber and Bowling 2004). In Britain, focus on Muslims as an internal security threat, most cogently depicted by the "home-grown-terrorist" category has dictated public expressions of terrorism since the 2005 London bombings. However, questions of Muslim loyalty have shifted during the Syrian conflict as British-born Muslims have travelled to fight alongside IS or Daesh in Syria (Awan and Guru 2017; Silverman 2017) including, as with the Manchester bomber, Salman Abedi, returning to enact violence at home having received training in Syria which has important implications for the perceptions of refugees from Syria and the region. The Muslim Other invokes the Gothic's concern with the disruption of spatial boundaries through association with globally diffuse terror networks as well as depictions of asylum seekers as threats to national security which feature in discourses of public protection and punishment (Valier 2002, 322). This article explores parallels between the securitization of Muslims within the "war on terror" context and construction of Syrian refugees as threats.

The Syrian refugee "crisis" has prompted contradictory responses of securitization of European borders on the one hand, and grassroots compassion on the other. The 2014 VPRS was implemented in response to "considerable pressure" (House of Commons 2017, 9) from charities, the United Nations High Commissioner for Refugees (UNHCR), and Houses of Parliament, and extended in 2015 to resettle 20,000 refugees from the Syrian region by 2020. Concerns ensued about their ability to integrate within western secular nations (Selby and Beaman 2016, 8). The 2015 Cologne sexual attacks and robberies on New Year's eve were problematically attributed to new Muslim migrant and refugee populations (Kingsley 2015; Ataç, Rygiel, and Stierl 2016, 528; Hoffmann et al. 2016), which fed into orientalist tropes of the sexually lascivious oriental male (Bhattacharyya 2008). Public discourses shifted from accommodation to concerns of "uncontrolled" migration, replaying the Gothic narrative of "reverse colonisation" whereby the nation is "vulnerable to attack from more vigorous, 'primitive' peoples" (Arata 1990, 623). Within populist and increasingly broader political spectrums, the refugee began to be "re-figured as the potential 'terrorist' who surreptitiously infiltrates the space of Europe," or as the "potential 'criminal' or 'rapist' who corrodes the social and moral fabric of 'Europe' from within" (New Keywords Collective 2016).

Following the 2015 and 2016 Paris terror attacks and backlash against refugees amid fears of Islamist terrorists exploiting refugee channels to enter Europe, as well as an upsurge in a populist nationalism and anti-Muslim rhetoric during the Brexit campaign and recent UK terror attacks, the figure of the Muslim exposes the persistence of racial thinking to imaginaries of Europe. Within this volatile context, this paper examines the limits of hospitality towards the Muslim Other and implications for refugee resettlement from conflicts in Syria and the region in the UK. I argue that state policy on refugee resettlement and counter-terrorism within the context of the Syrian war have increasingly become interpenetrated, meaning the "Muslim question" cannot be divorced from security concerns associated with terrorism and national identity. Important here is how discourses of "safety" are (re)formulated and point to complex (re)negotiations of belonging that challenge us to (re)consider not only what it means to be human, but what it means to be humane in a post-Brexit nation.

Conflating "the refugee" and "terrorist" categories: Muslims as conditional citizens

Since 9-11, trajectories of the "war on asylum" and "war on terrorism" have converged (Sivanandan 2006, 2) by collapsing categories of "asylum seeker" and "terrorist" (Weber and Bowling 2004, 198). Increasingly stringent immigration and anti-terrorism legislation comprise exclusionary practices of nation construction that Gothicise Muslims as a "different order of humanity" (Razack 2008, 7). For example, the UK Anti-Terrorism Crime and Security Act 2001 abolished habeas corpus and introduced detention without trial for foreign nationals.[1] Every (Muslim) immigrant or asylum seeker could be stopped and searched, legitimated on the basis of suspected links to international terrorism (Sivanandan 2006, 5), which derogated the European Convention on Human Rights (Collyer 2005). Terror tactics visited upon Muslims include deportation and deprivation of citizenship rights through introducing the 2006 Immigration, Asylum and Nationality Act alongside the "list of unacceptable behaviours" in the 2006 Terrorism Act. Right to remain for foreign nationals could be revoked, enabling the UK Government to "formalize the distinction between "moderate" and "extremist" Muslims in Britain" (McGhee 2008, 45).

Restrictions to citizenship rights have been extended to British Muslims through the Counter-Terrorism and Security Act 2015 which empowers police "to seize and retain passports" (c.6 Part1. Chapter 1) and tickets from those *suspected* of terrorist involvement and impose a Temporary Exclusion Order to "disrupt and control the return to the UK of British citizens who have engaged in terrorism-related activity abroad." Measures include cancelling travel documents and placing individuals on a "no fly" list, as well as enforcing restrictions on their return. Such measures are emboldened by a Gothic narrative of the Muslim Other terrorizing the civilized world expressed through the "specter of returning fighters" of IS (Joppke 2016, 728–729). The Gothic occupies the site of discursive struggle for societies to claim possession of the civilized by abjecting what is considered Other to the civilized self (Punter and Byron 2003, 5), which is evident in the arena of civil rights surrounding counter-terrorism measures. The Home Office (2018, 4, my italics) states that restrictions are "necessary in a *democratic* society" for national security, illustrating that Britain's claims to democratic (i.e. civilized) virtues are used to legitimise securitizing Muslims' bodies. Increased powers to deprive citizenship of those suspected of terrorist involvement and removing procedural safeguards creates a "hierarchy among British citizens" (Choudhury 2017, 225), specifically Muslims (Farques 2017, 984–985). As Choudhury explains:

> Muslims are at best "Tolerated Citizens", required to demonstrate their commitment to British values. Muslims holding unacceptable extremist views are "Failed Citizens" while the "home-grown" radicalised terrorist suspect is conceived of as the barbaric Other to British values, whose failure as a citizen is severe enough to justify the deprivation of citizenship.

Invocations of Muslims as Britain's "barbaric Other" or what Puar and Rai (2002) term, "terrorist-monsters," enables Gothic spaces of law where violence is simultaneously concealed within, yet performed by, modern law (Valier 2002, 333). These measures are evident of a "conditional order of hospitality" (Honig 2006, 112) for Muslims fundamental to Britain's contemporary "racial formation" (Kapoor 2013, 1029, 2018; also Kapoor and Narkowicz 2017) that privileges normative citizens' security above equality.

Muslims' transnational identification exceeds national borders (Khan 2006, 182–187), meaning the liberal state must contend not only with the domestic arena, but the "broader geopolitical structure of liberal hegemony" (Adamson, Triadafilopoulos, and Zolberg 2011, 848) arising from Britain's global position in the "war on terror," with implications for both countering terrorism and, as the next section examines, refugee resettlement.

Securitizing the refugee regime

This section explores how practices of racial biopolitics present in responses to resettling Syrian refugees operate through five features of the Concentrationary Gothic framework: (1) nation construction; (2) spatial control; (3) racial profiling and surveillance/screening practices; (4) restrictions to political engagement and freedom of speech; (5) production of internal divisions within the oppressed group.

The Syrian refugee "crisis" offers a significant terrain for addressing how "race" is deployed in nation construction to order and exclude populations. The Syrian Muslim represents Europe's constitutive outside, whose admittance would threaten the fundamental meaning of Europeanness. Exclusionary resettlement practices, notably Slovakia's outright refusal to accept Syrian Muslims on the basis that, as a Christian country it would be unable to accommodate them, highlights how Europeanness functions as a "defining logic of race" (Hesse 2007, 646) based on whiteness, Christianity, and modernity. Although ostensibly designed to resettle refugees arising from the war in Syria and the region, the UK government's VPRS reaffirms Muslims as Gothic others associated with illiberal and barbaric behaviours by centralizing minority identities (religious, gendered, disabled, sexuality) as priorities for humanitarian assistance, and therefore "'as' victims of the archetypal

Muslim other" (Fiddian-Qasmiyeh 2016; also Akram 2000) in need of modernization, democratization, and secularization. Kirtsoglou and Tsimouris (2016, 8) corroborate that portraying the Orient as "a space that breeds war, violence, persecution and poverty," produces Europe antithetically as developed and superior, importantly, "concealing its own responsibilities and geostrategic role in the staging of wars and violence." This representation justifies international intervention and exclusion/containment through reposing a central concern of the Gothic of "claiming possession of the civilized" by treating the Other as uncivilized (Punter and Byron 2003, 5).

I move on to discuss racialized practices of spatial control that designate spaces of un/safety. The UK government's decision to prioritise allocating humanitarian aid to Syria and the region rather than resettling Syrians in the UK highlights how constructions of safety are used politically to determine where right to reside can be granted. Humanitarian aid is presented as a means of protecting Syrians from making the "dangerous" (House of Commons 2017, 4) journey to Europe. An alternative reading is that it operates as a containment policy within the (European) "crisis" framework (Fiddian-Qasmiyeh 2016, 458), prolonging Syrians' risk by prioritizing UK citizens' security amid fears that Islamist terrorists will exploit refugee routes to perpetrate attacks within Europe. IS claimed responsibility for the November 2015 Paris attacks that killed 130 people and injured 368 as retaliation for French airstrikes on IS targets in Syria and Iraq. Planned in Syria and organized by a Belgium-based terrorist cell, the assailants were mostly French or Belgian citizens, two were Iraqi nationals, all had fought in Syria, and some had entered Europe amongst migrants and refugees seeking refuge.

Racialized conceptions of "could be terrorists" rely on established stereotypes which are reworked to fit contemporary treatment of refugees from Syria and the region. As Goldberg (2006, 345, original italics) observes, "The Muslim in Europe – not individual Muslims, not even Muslim communities, but *the idea* of the Muslim himself – has come to represent the threat of violent death." Not only does granting humanitarian aid enable the UK government to perform the role of benevolent benefactor, but it keeps Syrian refugees away from Britain. Examples include the European Commission proposing a European Border and Coast Guard on the 15 December 2015 to fortify Europe's external borders and Schengan area.

Practices of racial profiling and surveillance/screening reflect the Gothic's preoccupation with classifying "monstrous" bodies deemed threatening to the social order. The shift from human rights to security for determining refugee status contests the universalism to which claims to the category of the human worthy of protection can be forged. Significant infringements to human rights characterizing counter-terrorism measures during the "war on terror" (McGhee 2008, 111) are present in practices of securitization used in the VPRS, which encompass biometric and profile building to determine those suitable for resettlement in the UK. Cases are submitted by the UNHCR to be screened by the Home Office. Evidence given to the International Development Committee details the two-stage screening process for refugees considered for resettlement (House of Commons 2017, 19). Firstly, biometric details and bio-data are taken. Whilst Gilroy (2000, 108) argues that such technological innovations means that the individual "is even less constrained by the immediate forms of physical presence established by the body," I follow Pugliese's (2008, 49) critique of such post-racial accounts who argues that within the "war on terror," biometric technologies *secure* "identity dominance" by pre-emptively identifying, targeting and capturing suspects. Biometrics provide a similar function within the VPRS by pre-emptively excluding individuals from resettlement. Physical bodies, as Puar (2007, 151–159) contends in her discussion of counter-terrorism practices, are transformed into "data bodies," further illustrating how counter-terrorism measures and the refugee regime interpenetrate.

Subject to the white (non-Muslim) gaze, the potential refugee must meet the criteria for resettlement determined by their observer involving restrictions to freedom of speech and political engagement. As Arendt (1979, 299) argues, human rights is founded on a central dilemma since it presumes the existence of a universally determined "human being as such." However, for the refugee to be recognized *as a refugee* their subjecthood must be stripped back, meaning they are divested of agency, both political and social. For Syrian refugees, their political proclivities are used as screening criteria to secure the British subject from threat. The second stage involves building a profile about the potential refugee to be resettled; a practice comparable to the use of profiles in pre-emptive counter-terrorism policing. This involves: "go[ing]' out into communities in the region to understand who this person in front of them and applying is. They will, at that point, screen people out on the basis of criminality, combatants and war crime" (International Development Committee 2015). Collyer (2005, 283) explains that whilst "refugee" is a "morally unassailable category," "terrorist" "shifts the balance," legitimizing "repressive measures." Similar to differentiations operating within the UK "war on terror" context between "moderate" and "extremist," the moderate Muslim, as Tyrer (2008, 59) writes, refers to a "qualified Muslimness; a muted alterity" that depoliticizes them.

Internal divisions within the oppressed group are engendered because members must compete for recognition of victimhood, further subjecting them to the position of vulnerable. Asymmetric positioning of vulnerability/protector implied by the scheme's name (Syrian *Vulnerable* Person Relocation Scheme) and its stated priority of "helping the most *vulnerable* refugees who cannot be supported in the region" (House of Commons 2017, 9), reinforces conceptions of the refugee as a victim requiring saving. The potential refugee must perform a non-threatening "refugeeness" that corresponds to received understandings of the refugee as victim requiring protection, that in turn, enables UK state actors to take up a dominant position; a neo-colonial configuration of white benevolence or contemporary manifestation of the "white saviour." The figure of the refugee not only challenges conceptions of universal human rights therefore, but highlights "refugeeness" as a "site of contestation" (Suzuki 2016, 1) that supports neo-colonial practices of classification and exclusion.

I move on to discuss two contemporary examples that illustrate the human rights-security nexus framing responses to refugees from conflicts in Syria and the region.

"Breaking point": invasion and the "Muslim threat"

The controversial *Breaking Point* poster used by former UKIP leader, Nigel Farage, as part of the Leave campaign during the 2016 EU referendum in Britain played on fears of being invaded by asylum seekers that can be understood as a contemporary re-working of the "reverse colonisation" Gothic narrative linked to perceived decline of national and racial identity (Brantlinger 1988; Arata 1990). I discuss the poster because it presents a stark example of how race hate has been mobilized for political ends within the Brexit context and secondly, illustrates continuities in racial terror experienced by Jewish populations during World War 11 and colonial logics of subjection and exclusion that fit with the Concentrationary Gothic framework I am advancing.

The poster depicted lines of people largely from conflicts in Syria seeking refuge in Europe. Reported by David Prentis of the Unison Union to the Metropolitan Police for inciting racial hatred (*Guardian,* 16 June, 2016), the poster highlights how racialized logics were being used to cast Middle Eastern asylum seekers and the Muslim Other in particular, as a threat to Europe through recourse to familiar Gothic tropes of invasion that have historically been used to stir hatred against racialized populations deemed undesirable for inclusion within the national community (Tesfahuney 1998).

Of particular significance is how, rendered an anonymous mass of bodies, the poster visually depicts the racial epidermal schema of which Fanon (1986, 112) speaks, where the racialized Other is denied subjecthood. Rajaram (2002, 251) provides a fitting description of how refugees are "consigned to the body. That is, they are rendered speechless and without agency, a physical entity, or rather a physical *mass* within which individuality is subsumed. Corporeal, refugees are speechless and consigned to 'visuality' ... ." In contrast, Farage's uniqueness is foregrounded. As a normative white male, he can occupy the role of speaking subject who re-casts the individual experiences of those featured as an opportunity for reproducing exclusionary racial technologies well-placed to determine which bodies are suitable for inclusion within the (normative white) national imaginary. As Goldberg (2009, 1273) reminds us, racism is not reducible to "narrow connections to colonial subjection and repression, ordering and governmentality." Rather, colonial outlooks continue to inform conditions of possibility for exploiting, governing and admitting or excluding those categorized as racially different and by contrast, elevating those understood as racially belonging to the dominant and privileged.

There are two key aspects concerning the human rights-security nexus which I want to elaborate. Firstly, how the Concentrationary Gothic framework sensitizes us to how current racial configurations operating within the refugee regime and their interrelation with Gothic tropes draw from earlier terror formations. In support of a relational approach that "seeks to *connect* racial logics" (Meer 2013b, 501, original italics), the Gothic draws attention to how representational frameworks shift depending on which group is charged with harbouring uncivilized or barbarous tendencies that make them unsuitable for inclusion. Racial conceptions and racist practices, although local in terms of their resonances and meaning, nonetheless exhibit ties to wider circulations of meaning across time and place (Goldberg 2009, 1273). Debate has ensued concerning the relationship between anti-semitism and Islamophobia and "the place of ... race in relation to religion" (Rana 2007, 150; also Meer 2013a). Current depictions of the Muslim Other invading Europe demonstrate historical continuities with anti-semitism and Gothicisation of the figure of the Jew. The trope of invasion and its semantic association with the parasite present in anti-semitism in nineteenth century England was reflected in Gothic narratives of the time and the figure of the nationless Wandering Jew (Shapiro 1997; Davison 2004) emblematic of the Jewish question. Halberstam notes (1995, 14) that the Jew was "marked as a threat to capital, to masculinity, and to nationhood." The poster illustrates how the concentrationary seeps into, and shapes, contemporary racial configurations and intersects with Gothic discourses, whereby racialized groups are constructed as threats to the health of the nation. It was not long before comparisons were being made with a Nazi propaganda film (*Guardian*, 16 June, 2016) depicting unwanted Jewish refugees during World War Two seeking refuge with subtitles on the historic image describing them as "parasites undermining their host countries." In the current context, the refugee figured as Muslim is articulated through a comparable discourse of white dispossession centred on a loss of national identity following the admittance of refugees into Britain.

Secondly, the poster invites us to consider, at the heart of racialized biopolitical regimes and terror formations on which they are premised, whose human rights should be protected, or, put another way, whose lives can be put at risk? Converging terrors of terrorism and loss of national identity occupying western societies post-9/11, and which have regained momentum following recent terror attacks within European cities, can be understood through the Gothic's preoccupation with borders and their collapse. The

Gothic nature of contemporary social risks (forthcoming; also Valier 2002, Abbas 2013) arises from a fundamental concern with security both "national security and personal ontological security" (McGhee 2005, 76). What has surfaced in the post-9/11 context is a Gothic populism that draws into relation a pronounced "asylophobia" (McGhee 2005, 76) with the threat of terrorism (Weber and Bowling 2004, 198). Depicting "Middle Eastern looking" refugees en masse as security threats divorces them from their particular histories of flight, including how these displacements are in part a result of UK foreign policy and places the rights of UK citizens above those of asylum seekers. Although the Syrian War predates the so-called refugee "crisis" and Brexit, it only becomes framed as a "crisis" when the borders separating Europe from its Muslim Others are disrupted (see James, this issue). The presence of refugees arising from conflicts in Syria and the region thus re-centres the question of whose life counts as a human life?

White dispossession and the threat of the Syrian "man-child"

The second example explores how admittance of child refugees from countries including Syria and Afghanistan following the dissolution of the Calais "Jungle" is framed as a potential security risk that requires that the refugee subject their body for scrutiny, again illustrating a racialized biopolitics premised on classifying bodies to be protected/excluded. Conceived within the Concentrationary Gothic framework, I argue that these biopolitical practices draw their legitimacy from the Gothic figure of the "man-child;" that is of the (male) asylum seeker posing as a child to gain entry to the UK. This figure articulates fears of the Muslim posing a security risk to the normative white populace by illegally entering Britain's borders through false or mistaken identity (a key Gothic trope) and exploiting Britain's hospitality. It provides a useful entryway for examining how categories of the "human" are being fought within the contemporary context of the "Muslim question" and how practices of racialization and Gothicisation intersect (Abbas 2013, forthcoming; also Malchow 1996, 4). This figure can be understood as a recent manifestation of longstanding racialized tropes of the deceitful Arab that reanimates the Gothic discourse of degeneration by embodying the threat of the nation collapsing into barbarity and chaos (Hurley 1996, 10; Byron 2000, 132–133), as the Cologne attacks described earlier have etched into the popular imaginary. The Gothic maps an alternative trajectory to the certainties of science for determining the presence of criminality and thus securing the subject; here figured by the "man-child" whose potential indetermination poses alarm. This figure embodies an important departure between the Gothic and Enlightenment science described by Wagner (2012, 75) whereby "In contrast to scientific faith in the transparent body," the body is represented in the Gothic as "an untrustworthy source of information about the self."

70   RACIAL NATIONALISMS

To illustrate this figure, I refer to an article in the *Express* (19 October 2016) which reports on the media row on admittance of child refugees following a caller's "furious tirade at the liberal elite" for opting to censor pictures of child migrants arriving in the UK. The article has been chosen because although I am not making claims to its representativeness, it provides a useful illustration of how the Brexit context has shaped attitudes to refugee resettlement. Further, it highlights important intersections of "race" and class whereby the white nationalist takes up the position of a dispossessed white subject threatened not only by the presence of ("Muslim looking") refugees, but subscribers to a liberal discourse by white elites that contravenes the rights of white working class Britons.

In an interesting move in which the *BBC* liberal elite are constituted as the parasitic object feeding off the white working poor, a caller, known only as Tony from Liverpool, berates the *BBC* for censoring the faces of child refugees arriving in the UK from the Calais Jungle, preventing viewers from deciding for themselves if they are actually children deserving Britain's hospitality. Positioning himself as a taxpayer, and thus legitimate citizen and contributor to the nation, Tony is affronted by the duping he believes white working class Britons have been subjected to by what he terms, "liberal elites," depicted as out of touch with the realities of a disenfranchized white populace. Tony indicates that the EU referendum provided an opportunity to regain power for ordinary Britons by forcing elites to address the concerns of those usually disregarded – the white working class: "If they [politicians] learned anything from the referendum over the EU it is that if you want to try and fool the people, you go ahead and do that but it will cost you at the ballot box," he rants.

Admittance of Syrian refugee children is presented as another instance in which white working class Britons are being exploited into giving up resources of which they already have little share. Debates concerning differentiating the (illegitimate) economic migrant from the "rightful refugee" to be protected, effectively pits the refugee against the white working class citizen as a threat to their economic security, which not only fuels antagonisms towards refugees, but exposes the limits of hospitality towards refugee resettlement. As Sales (2002) notes, increasingly stringent asylum policy has created "a new social category of asylum seeker … portrayed as 'undeserving' in contrast to the 'deserving' refugee." Politicization of asylum issues concerning welfare provision and increased controls on legal entry to "Fortress Europe" has strengthened asylum seekers' association with a burden on welfare *and* as "illegals." Criminalization of the asylum seeker has particular significance for Middle Eastern claimants through their association with terrorism.

The shift from human rights to security enables the normative white subject to take up the position of being "at risk" from a "threatening Other," limiting refugees' humanity from being protected or even recognized. Invoking the dangerousness of the refugee, Tory MP David Davies is quoted in the article as saying "The UK has set a very dangerous precedent," whereby people can claim they are under 18 and have relatives in the UK and be accepted. Differentiating the legitimate refugee from the "undeserving" involves reducing the refugee to the body, and even further, to their constituent body parts. This is most starkly displayed in the 2016 furore concerning using dental X-rays to determine the ages of children seeking refuge which brought the issue of human rights to the fore. The British Dental Association was adamant in its condemnation on ethical grounds to such measures being enforced.[2] Framing refugees as security threats requiring "verification" exposes the shift in focus from granting human rights to assessing security risk. Yet as the previous example showed, this re-focusing is a re-assertion of racial dominance rather than new territory.

Necessity for the racialized Other to be "known," underpinning Tony's demand to see the refugees' faces, shows how refusal to represent the Other disrupts racial dynamics of looking where, following Fanon (1986, 110), the racialized Other is forced to "meet the white man's eyes." Spurr (1993, 14) describes how "looking and speaking enter into the economy of an essentially colonial situation, in which one race holds, however provisionally and uneasily, authority over another." Inability to see the Other thus undermines the authority of the white nationalist, inciting an angered desire to regain power and control considered rightfully theirs.

Performances of exclusion undertaken by Brexiters highlight contestations not only between white nationalists and minority communities, but between white working class populations and white elites. Such conflicts illustrate not only the importance of class to articulations of racism, but the salience of whiteness for understanding how relations of racism are (re)configured and operate at a number of levels of antagonism within the Brexit context. The indeterminate figure of the man-child comprises what Halberstam (2000, 21, 22) terms a "Gothic technology" by condensing multiple fears relating to nationality, race, class, and gender in one body, and by contrast, produces the normative human as white, male, and middle-class. Since the body is a key instrument of discipline (Wagner 2012), dissolution of the boundaries of the body and self pose a threat to the social order.

In her excellent discussion of fin-de-siècle Gothic, Hurley (1996, 3) notes its obsession with "the ruination of the human subject," where in place of a stable, bounded human subject, is instead the "spectacle of body metamorphic and undifferentiated." Difficulties in ascertaining the "real refugee" who in this example, fools others by pretending to be a vulnerable child, legitimates dehumanizing screening practices to be undertaken for us to recognize them as humans worthy of our protection. As such, questions of the human are inextricably linked to that of the humane. The act of accepting refugees – a humane act – is nonetheless conditioned by inhumane activities that are legitimized in order to protect humanity, but which point to the ever-present possibility of the ruination of the human subject.

Conclusion

This article has explored the seismic shift from viewing asylum through the lens of human rights to security. Conflation of trajectories of asylum and counter-terrorism within the context of the Syrian conflict has particular implications for securing sanctuary within the UK for Muslim refugees arising from these conflicts. I advanced the Concentrationary Gothic as a framework for understanding how racialized practices of nation construction, spatial control, racial profiling and surveillance/screening practices, restrictions to freedom of speech and political engagement, and internal divisions produced within the oppressed group, are legitimated by Gothic discourses that present Muslims as uncivilized and barbarous beings who pose a threat to national security and identity.

The VPRS illustrates continuities in logics of racial terror visited upon the Muslim refugee through racialized biopolitical technologies. Racialized screening strategies involving profile building and biometrics and biodata to assess whether individuals are "risky" are comparable to preventative counter-terrorism measures that produce both as suspect populations, and further, perpetuate a racialized hierarchy of humans where safety is not secured, but must be recognized and earned. This requires that Syrian refugees subject their body for scrutiny and submit personal narratives that are palatable to the demands of western democratic states by performing a depoliticized and non-threatening self, thus perpetuating neo-colonial configurations of vulnerable/protector.

The Concentrationary Gothic is attentive to relational logics of race/racism (Goldberg 2009) that traverse time and space. I analysed two recent examples of the treatment of Middle Eastern refugees to illustrate how existing racialized tropes have been re-worked to suit current socio-political conditions. Representations of refugees as parasitic invaders feeding off the populace as depicted in the *Breaking Point* poster and its historic evil twin, the Nazi propaganda video, illustrate the importance of drawing together concentrationary and Gothic frameworks to conceptualize how racial terror draws its impulses from previous articulations of threat, invasion, insecurity, and monstrosity to justify contemporary conditions of domination and curtailment of human rights present in exclusionary border tactics and racial profiling within the Syrian refugee "crisis." I advanced the figure of the "man-child" as a recent manifestation of the deceitful Arab that draws together Gothic and racialized discourses to produce Middle Eastern asylum seekers as a threat to the UK populace. These depictions legitimise dehumanizing screening practices to determine the ages of asylum seekers in order to protect the security of the (white) nation. Exemplified by the Concentrationary Gothic framework, the figure of the refugee highlights that the category of "human" is not secured; recognition *as human* is required for safety and security to be granted and further, that this category is imbricated within racialized power structures meaning hospitality is always foreshadowed by the possibility of hostility to the Other.

Notes

1. Indefinite detention of foreign nationals without trial was ruled discriminatory by the Law Lords in 2004. Then Home Secretary, Charles Clarke, subsequently introduced the Prevention of Terrorism Act 2005 which replaced detention without trial with control orders (electronic tagging and house arrests).
2. The Home Office ruled out dental checks used to verify the ages of refugees arriving from Calais in October 2016 as "inaccurate, inappropriate and unethical." However, the Home Office stated that "physical appearance and demeanour are used as part of the interview process" by UK and French officials to "assess age." On arrival to Britain, refugee children are fingerprinted as "part of further identity checks" (*Guardian,* 19 October 2016).

Disclosure statement

No potential conflict of interest was reported by the author.

ORCID

Madeline-Sophie Abbas ⓘ http://orcid.org/0000-0002-0426-1924

References

Abbas, M.-S. 2013. "'White Terror in the War on Terror." *Critical Race and Whiteness Studies e-Journal* 9 (1). https://www.academia.edu/5057776/White_.
Abbas, M.-S. forthcoming. *Terror and the Dynamism of Islamophobia in 21st Century Britain: The Concentrationary Gothic.* Basingstoke: Palgrave Macmillan.
Adamson, F. B., T. Triadafilopoulos, and A. R. Zolberg. 2011. "The Limits of the Liberal State: Migration, Identity and Belonging in Europe." *Journal of Ethnic and Migration Studies* 37 (6): 843–859. doi:10.1080/1369183X.2011.576188.
Agamben, G. 1998. *Homo Sacer: Sovereign Power and Bare Life.* Stanford: Stanford University Press.
Akram, S. M. 2000. "Orientalism Revisited in Asylum and Refugee Claims." *International Journal of Refugee Law* 12 (1): 7–40. doi:10.1093/ijrl/12.1.7
Arata, S. 1990. "The Occidental Tourist: *Dracula* and the Anxiety of Reverse Colonization." *Victorian Studies* 33 (4): 621–645.
Arendt, H. 1979. *The Origins of Totalitarianism.* New York: Harcourt Brace & Company.
Ataç, I., K. Rygiel, and M. Stierl. 2016. "Introduction: The Contentious Politics of Refugee and Migrant Protest and Solidarity Movements: Remaking Citizenship

from the Margins." *Citizenship Studies* 20 (5): 527–544. doi:10.1080/13621025.2016.1182681.

Awan, I., and S. Guru. 2017. "Parents of Foreign "Terrorist" Fighters in Syria – Will They Report Their Young?" *Ethnic and Racial Studies* 40 (1): 24–42. doi:10.1080/01419870.2016.1206588.

Bhattacharyya, G. 2008. *Dangerous Brown Men: Exploiting Sex, Violence and Feminism in the War on Terror*. London: Zed Books.

Brantlinger, P. 1988. *Rules of Darkness: British Literature and Imperialism, 1830-1914*. Ithaca and London: Cornell University Press.

Byron, G. 2000. "Gothic in the 1890s." In *A Companion to the Gothic*, edited by D. Punter, 132–142. Oxford: Blackwells.

Cantle, T. 2001. *Community Cohesion: A Report of the Independent Review Team*. London: Home Office.

Casey, L. 2016. *The Casey Review: A Review into Opportunity and Integration*. London: Crown Copyright.

Choudhury, T. 2017. "The Radicalisation of Citizenship Deprivation." *Critical Social Policy* 37 (2): 225–244. doi:10.1177/0261018316684507.

Collyer, M. 2005. "Secret Agents: Anarchists, Islamists and Responses to Politically Active Refugees in London." *Ethnic and Racial Studies* 28 (2): 278–303. doi:10.1080/01419870420000315852.

Davison, C. M. 2004. *Anti-Semitism and British Gothic Literature*. New York: Palgrave Macmillan.

Express. 2016. "LBC Caller Launches FURIOUS TIRADE at the 'Liberal Elite' Media Over Row on Child Refugees." 19 October. https://www.express.co.uk/news/uk/722834/lbc-caller-rant-child-calais-jungle-refugees-liberal-elite-bbc.

Fanon, F. 1986. *Black Skin White Masks*. London: Pluto Press.

Fargues, É. 2017. "The Revival of Citizenship Deprivation in France and the UK as an Instance of Citizenship Renationalisation." *Citizenship Studies* 21 (8): 984–998. doi:10.1080/13621025.2017.1377152.

Fiddian-Qasmiyeh, E. 2016. "Repressentations of Displacement in the Middle East." *Public Culture* 28 (3): 457–473.

Gilroy, P. 2000. *Between Camps: Nations, Cultures, and the Allure of Race*. London and New York: Routledge.

Glover, D. 1996. *Vampires, Mummies and Liberals: Bram Stoker and the Politics of Popular Fiction*. Durham: Duke University Press.

Goldberg, D. T. 2006. "Racial Europeanization." *Ethnic and Racial Studies* 29 (2): 331–364.

Goldberg, D. T. 2009. "Racial Comparisons, Relational Racisms: Some Thoughts on Method." *Ethnic and Racial Studies* 32 (7): 1271–1282.

Guardian. 2016. "Home Office Expected to Speed up Rescue of Migrant Children from Calais." 19 October. https://www.theguardian.com/world/2016/oct/19/home-office-expected-to-speed-up-rescue-of-migrant-children-from-calais.

Guardian. 2016. "Nigel Farage's Anti-Migrant Poster Reported to Police." 16 June. https://www.theguardian.com/politics/2016/jun/16/nigel-farage-defends-ukip-breaking-point-poster-queue-of-migrants.

Hage, G. 1998. *White Nation: Fantasies of Supremacy in a Multicultural Society*. Annadale: Pluto Press.

Halberstam, J. 1995. *Skin Shows: Gothic Horror and the Technology of Monsters*. Durham and London: Duke University Press.

Halberstam, J. 2000. *Skin Shows: Gothic Horror and the Technology of Monsters*. Durham and London: Duke University Press.

Hesse, B. 2007. "Racialized Modernity: An Analytics of White Mythologies." *Ethnic and Racial Studies* 30 (4): 643–663.

Hoffmann, C., J. Jüttner, S. Kempf, A.-K. Müller, C. Schmergal, K. Thimm, and A. Ulrich. 2016. "Sexism and Islam Debated in Germany after Cologne Attacks." *Der Spiegel*, 28 January.

Home Office. 2018. "Counter Terrorism and Security Bill: European Convention on Human Rights Memorandum." Bills (14–15) 059. Accessed January 26, 2018. www.parliament.uk/documents/joint-committees/human-rights/ECHR_Memo_Counter_terrorism_Bill.pdf.

Honig, B. 2006. "Another Cosmopolitanism: Law and Politics in the New Europe." In *Democracy and Difference: Contesting the Boundaries of the Political*, edited by S. Benhabib, 257–277. Princeton: Princeton University Press.

House of Commons. 2017. *The UK Response to the Syrian Refugee Crisis*. Briefing paper 06805, 14 June. http://researchbriefings.files.parliament.uk/documents/SN06805/SN06805.pdf.

Hurley, K. 1996. *The Gothic Body: Sexuality, Materialism and Degeneration at the Fin de Siècle*. Cambridge: Cambridge University Press.

Huysmans, J. 1995. "Migrants as a Security Problem: Dangers of 'Securitizing' Societal Issues." In *Migration and European Integration: The Dynamics of Inclusion and Exclusion*, edited by R. Miles, and D. Thränhardt, 53–72. London: Pinter Publishers.

Independent. 2016. "Jo Cox 'Was Preparing Report on Far-Right Nationalists and Rise of Islamophobia'." 20 June. https://www.independent.co.uk/news/uk/home-news/jo-cox-was-preparing-report-on-far-right-nationalists-a7090981.html.

International Development Committee. 2015. Oral Evidence, Syrian Refugee Crisis, 17 November. HC 463 2015-16, Q74.

Joppke, C. 2016. "Terror and the Loss of Citizenship." *Citizenship Studies* 20 (6-7): 728–748. doi:10.1080/13621025.2016.1191435.

Kapoor, N. 2013. "The Advancement of Racial Neoliberalism in Britain." *Ethnic and Racial Studies* 36 (6): 1028–1046. doi:10.1080/01419870.2011.629002.

Kapoor, N. 2018. *Deport, Deprive, Extradite: 21st Century State Extremism*. London: Verso.

Kapoor, N., and K. Kasia Narkowicz. 2017. "Unmaking Citizens: Passport Removals, Preemptive Policing and the Reimagining of Colonial Governmentalities." *Ethnic and Racial Studies* 42: 45–62.

Khan, S. 2006. "Muslims!." In *A Postcolonial People: South Asians in Britain*, edited by N. Ali, V. S. Kara, and S. Sayyid, 182–187. London: Hurst.

Kingsley, P. 2015. "Why Syrian Refugee Passport Found at Paris Attack Scene Must be Treated with Caution." *The Guardian*, 15 November.

Kirtsoglou, E., and E. Tsimouris. 2016. "'Il était un petit navire' The refugee crisis, neo-orientalism, and the production of radical alterity." *Journal of Modern Greek Studies* Occasional Paper 9: 1–14.

Malchow, H. L. 1996. *The Gothic and Images of Race in Nineteenth-Century Britain*. Stanford: Stanford University Press.

Mandaville, P. 2017. "Designating Muslims: Islam in the Western Policy Imagination." *The Review of Faith & International Affairs* 15 (3): 54–65. doi:10.1080/15570274.2017.1354466.

Marfleet, P. 2012. "Religion and Refuge." In *Secularism, Racism and the Politics of Belonging*, edited by N. Yuval-Davis, and P. Marfleet, 69–72. London: Runnymede Trust. https://www.runnymedetrust.org/uploads/publications/pdfs/Secularism%20RacismAndThePoliticsOfBelonging-2012.pdf.

Mbembe, A. 2003. "Necropolitics." *Public Culture* 15 (1): 11–40.

McGhee, D. 2005. *Intolerance Britain?: Hate, Citizenship and Difference*. Maidenhead: Open University Press.

McGhee, D. 2008. *The End of Multiculturalism?: Terrorism, Integration and Human Rights*. Maidenhead: Open University Press.

Meer, N. 2013a. "Racialization and Religion: Race, Culture and Difference in the Study of Antisemitism and Islamophobia." *Ethnic and Racial Studies* 36 (3): 385–398. doi:10.1080/01419870.2013.734392.

Meer, N. 2013b. "Semantics, Scales and Solidarities in the Study of Anti-Semitism and Islamophobia." *Ethnic and Racial Studies* 36 (3): 500–515. doi:10.1080/01419870.2013.734382.

Mighall, R. 1999. *A Geography of Victorian Gothic Fiction: Mapping History's Nightmares*. Oxford: Oxford University Press.

New Keywords Collective. 2016. "Europe/Crisis: New Keywords of 'the Crisis' in and of 'Europe.'" http:// nearfuturesonline.org/europecrisis-new-keywords-of-crisis-in-and-of-europe/.

Pollock, G., and M. Silverman. 2011. "Introduction: Concentrationary Cinema." In *Concentrationary Cinema: Aesthetics as Political Resistance in Alain Resnais's Night and fog (1955)*, edited by Griselda Pollock, and Max Silverman, 1–54. New York: Berghahn.

Pollock, G., and M. Silverman. 2014. "Introduction – The Politics of Memory: From Concentrationary Memory to Concentrationary Memories." In *Concentrationary Memories: Totalitarian Terror and Cultural Resistance*, edited by Griselda Pollock, and Max Silverman, 1–30. London: I. B. Tauris.

Puar, J. R. 2007. *Terrorist Assemblages: Homonationalism in Queer Times*. Durham: Duke University Press.

Puar, J. R., and A. S. Rai. 2002. "Monster, Terrorist, Fag: The War on Terrorism and the Production of Docile Patriots." *Social Text* 20 (3): 117–148.

Pugliese, J. 2008. "Biotypologies of Terrorism." *Cultural Studies Review* 14 (2): 49–66.

Punter, D., and G. Byron. 2003. *The Gothic*. Oxford: Blackwell Publishing.

Rajaram, P. K. 2002. "Humanitarianism and Representations of the Refugee." *Journal of Refugee Studies* 15 (3): 247–264. doi:10.1093/jrs/15.3.247.

Rana, J. 2007. "The Story of Islamophobia." *Souls* 9 (2): 148–162.

Razack, S. H. 2008. *Casting Out: The Eviction of Muslims from Western Law and Politics*. Toronto: University of Toronto Press.

Rousset, D. 1946. *L'Univers concentrationnaire* [The Concentrationary Universe]. Paris: Editions de Pavois.

Said, E. 2003. *Orientalism*. London: Penguin Books.

Sales, R. 2002. "The Deserving and the Undeserving? Refugees, Asylum Seekers and Welfare in Britain." *Critical Social Policy* 22 (3): 456–478.

Schmitt, C. 1997. *Alien Nation: Nineteenth-Century Gothic Fictions and English Nationality*. Philadelphia: University of Pennsylvania Press.

Selby, J. A., and L. G. Beaman. 2016. "Re-posing the "Muslim Question"." *Critical Research on Religion* 4 (1): 8–20. doi:10.1177/2050303216630541.

Shapiro, S. 1997. "The Uncanny Jew: A Brief History of an Image." *Judaism* 46 (1): 63–78.

Silverman, T. 2017. "U.K. Foreign Fighters to Syria and Iraq: The Need for a Real Community Engagement Approach." *Studies in Conflict & Terrorism* 40 (12): 1091–1107. doi:10.1080/1057610X.2016.1253991.

Sivanandan, A. 2006. "Race, Terror and Civil Society." *Race & Class* 47 (3): 1–8. doi:06108310.1177/0306396806061083.

Spurr, D. 1993. *The Rhetoric of Empire: Colonial Discourse in Journalism, Travel Writing, and Imperial Administration*. Durham and London: Duke UP.

Suzuki, M. 2016. "Performing the Human: Refugees, the Body, and the Politics of Universalism." *Refugee Studies Centre Working Paper Series* 117. file:///C:/Users/Home/AppData/Local/Packages/Microsoft.MicrosoftEdge_8wekyb3d8bbwe/TempState/Downloads/wp117-performing-the-human-2016.pdf.

Tell MAMA. 2017. A Constructed Threat: Identity, Prejudice and the Impact of Anti-Muslim Hatred Annual Report 2016. https://tellmamauk.org/wp-content/uploads/2017/11/A-Constructed-Threat-Identity-Intolerance-and-the-Impact-of-Anti-Muslim-Hatred-Web.pdf.

Tesfahuney, M. 1998. "Mobility, Racism and Geopolitics." *Political Geography* 17 (5): 499–515. doi.org/10.1016/S0962-6298(97)00022-X.

TUC. 2016. *Challenging Racism after the EU Referendum*. https://www.tuc.org.uk/sites/default/files/ChallengingracismaftertheEUreferendum2.pdf.

Tyrer, D. 2008. "The Unbearable Whiteness of Seeing: Moderated Muslims, (in)/Visibilities and Islamophobia." Thinking Thru' Islamophobia/A Symposium, pp.48–53. http://www.sociology.leeds.ac.uk/assets/files/research/cers/Islamophobia%20Symposium%20Papers%20e-working%20paper%20(3).pdf.

Valier, C. 2002. "Punishment, Border Crossings and the Powers of Horror." *Theoretical Criminology* 6 (3): 319–337.

Wagner, C. 2012. "The Dream of a Transparent Body: Identity, Science and the Gothic Novel." *Gothic Studies* 14 (1): 74–92. doi.org/10.7227/GS.14.1.8.

Weber, L., and B. Bowling. 2004. "Policing Migration: A Framework for Investigating the Regulation of Global Mobility." *Policing and Society* 14 (3): 195–212. doi:10.1080/1043946042000241802.

Care and cruelty in Chios: the "refugee crisis" and the limits of Europe

Malcolm James

ABSTRACT

Focusing on Chios, at the start of 2016, and my experience there as a volunteer, this paper aims to understand the forms of violence that unfolded in that location and considers what they mean for the social and political transformation of Europe. Violence takes many forms, but in this paper I focus on cruelty – specifically, modern, colonial and racial acts of excessive violence committed without regard for the victim. Secondly, the paper develops a feminist and postcolonial analysis of care. This analysis is concerned with acts of empathy, responsibility and relation that acted as correctives to cruelty. The paper shows how cruelty and care are intertwined and how their quotidian workings reveal wider patterns of violence and responsibility. However, rather than reiterate that care is ensnared in cruelty, this paper defends care's autonomy, vitality and centrality to an alternative humanist ethics.

From the end of 2015, the "refugee crisis" and the cruelty that accompanied it became mainstream news. Across Europe, borders were closed. In Calais, Hungary and on the Greek-Macedonian border severe violence against refugees was documented. In Brussels, an EU-Turkey deal was penned and long-standing asylum policy seemingly contravened. We saw the construction of refugee detention centres, abandoned children and Britain's commitment to offer nothing beyond the most minimal sanctuary to people it had actively displaced.

"Crisis" connotes novelty or brevity but what is happening is neither new nor will end soon. What has come to Europe's attention from the end of 2015 is the only the most recent phase of forced human displacement. In 2014, UNHCR (the UN body responsible for refugees) had reported that the world's forcibly displaced population stood at 56.5 million people – the largest since records began (2015). This was nineteen million more than a decade earlier. Although 86 per cent live in the Global South, the conflicts in Syria, Iraq and Afghanistan have driven increasing numbers to Spain, Italy and Greece. Here, at the southern limits of Europe, they were joined by other refugees – people forcibly displaced from their homes by free market trade agreements, land appropriation, ecological decline and by the wars in Somalia and Ukraine.[1]

Those arriving in Europe, encountered another crisis not of their making. Between 2007 and 2008, the financial crisis had led to a downturn in European fortunes, and against prevailing economic advice austerity had been rolled out (Krugman 2015). The European Commission, European Central Bank, Britain, and southern European countries informed their populations they would have to make do with less – less welfare and fewer public services.

In Greece, of which Chios is part, the financial crisis had an even heavier toll. There, austerity was rapid and deeply felt. Led by Germany, a group of actors (the European Central Bank, the International Monetary Fund and the Eurogroup) imposed a series of financial bailouts under strict austerity conditions. Under those conditions, public spending was slashed and the economy stagnated. Unemployment rose to 25 per cent and nearly half the Greek population fell below the poverty line (European Commission 2018). This was compounded by the loss of income from tourism. Holidaymakers across Europe were travelling less, and Greece's tourist destinations, such as Chios, felt it.

In this economic and social context, Chios, along with neighbouring islands Samos and Lesbos, became among the largest recipients of refugees in Europe. Geographically, politically and economically at the limits of Europe, Chios became a frontier for human displacement as it also became the testing grounds for aggressive neoliberal economic reforms. These activities were not marginal to the continent; rather they defined its centre. As Balibar had earlier noted, if Europe is defined by its political problems, "Greece is one of its centers, not because of the mythical origins of our civilization … but because of the current problems concentrated there" (2004, 2).

Focusing on Chios at the start of 2016 and my experience as a volunteer in that location, this paper addresses a small part of this story, and it does so with two specific purposes.[2] Firstly, in the context of the "refugee crisis", the paper aims to understand the forms of violence that unfolded in that location and considers what they mean for the social and political transformation of Europe. Violence can take many forms but in this paper I specifically focus on cruelty – acts of excessive violence committed without regard for the victim. This was the form of violence most evident on Chios.

Secondly, the paper develops an analysis of care. This analysis is concerned with acts of empathy, responsibility and relation that acted as correctives to cruelty. The paper shows how cruelty and care were intertwined and how

80 RACIAL NATIONALISMS

these quotidian workings revealed wider patterns of violence and responsibility unravelling at the time. However, rather than reiterate that care is ensnared in cruelty, this paper defends care's autonomy, vitality and centrality to an alternative humanist ethics.

To assist in this discussion of care and cruelty, the paper has been organized in accordance with the refugees' movement through the island. Whereas a more scientifically derived organization might separate out interlocking factors into discrete conceptual categories, this paper's intention is to show how narratives, histories, bureaucracies, practices, geographies and legislation intersected unevenly across the island, and to evaluate the presence of care and cruelty therein.

Cruelty and care

To open up the necessary analytic angles for this paper, I start by developing the concepts of cruelty and care.

Cruelty is a form of violence that causes excessive harm or pain to another, for which the perpetrator feels no culpability. This could be the pain caused by a torturer or by a face-less bureaucracy, and in this sense cruelty can be wilful at the same time as it is banal, routinized and inscribed into everyday practices. In Chios, it predominantly took the later form and was found in the interlinked narratives, histories, practices, bureaucracy, legislation, and spatial arrangement of the island.

The particular characteristics of these routinized cruelties are products of the development of modern Europe and its technologies and methods for controlling the human condition (Foucault 1977). In seeming contradiction, this modern formation of cruelty has run alongside the development of liberal human rights. Liberal human rights have as a central imperative the elimination of cruelty. So, cruelty has been institutionalized alongside a moral and ethical commitment to non-cruelty (Asad 2003, 109).

Within this, what has been considered, or not, to be cruel has been a matter of social definition. In the history of modern and colonial Europe, cruel behaviour has been deemed normal, necessary and even beneficial when it is socially sanctioned (Montaigne [1580] 1993). Whether it be the murderous judgements about the relative closeness of people to God made by the Spanish and Portuguese invaders of the Americas, the extent to which you are permitted to starve to death in the colonies, the poisoning of your waterways, or sterilization, who or who cannot be treated cruelly has always been determined by your closeness to Europe's ideal moral subject, and that distance has overwhelmingly been established by racism.

These racially determined cruelties have frequently taken on a colonial formation. While the systems of cruelty that operate within Europe today might not be seen as colonial – supposing that Europe cannot colonize itself – we should be clear that they are precisely that. It is in fact well documented that the forms of racial cruelty developed to such destructive ends in Europe in the 1940s, were pioneered in the colonies. There they acquired distinctively modern features corresponding with the management, surveillance and categorization of people, as they accrued colonial and racial forms of spatial and human arrangement (Cesaire 1972, 36). Powerfully amplified by Nazism and Stalinism but inherent to all modern European societies, the carnivalesque of medieval violence was then incorporated into modern Europe alongside these colonial and racial systems of order and control. This is what Bhabha, drawing on Walter Benjamin, refers to as the barbarism of modernity (2008).

While the formation of Europe has ensured many of these racial, colonial and modern cruelties are routinized in social and political life, those that stretch social acceptability require special discursive and legislative framings (Schmitt 2008). In Chios, this occurred through the extraordinary measures evoked by the European Council, measures which drew historical parallels with a state of siege – one form of the state of exception (European Council 2016). The mass killing of refugees at sea and the construction of detention facilities were not then part of the usual operation of life and death on the island. While a normal civilian constitution remained (unlike a state of emergency), legislation expanded to sanction unusual cruelties. Here, the military started to play a more significant role, alongside the police, in the securitization of the island, raising internal and external fortifications.

Those formations of cruelty were intertwined with care. In humanitarian literature, care is often developed through a Foucauldian framework which emphasizes its entrapment in institutionalized cruelty. Texts in this field address the blurred distinction between the hand that cares (the humanitarian world) and the hand that strikes (the police and military), noting the functional relationship of both in the management of undesirable people (Agier 2011, 5; Fassin 2005, 382). These texts are useful because they help think through the located intensities of cruelty and care, and what they mean, but they are also limited in that care is always captured in the tentacles of modern management.

Feminist and postcolonial scholarship is also concerned with how care can be contradictory. Here, care is intertwined with cruelty but is not reduced to it. Rather, it acts as a corrective sometimes maintaining humanity within systems of crushing racialized cruelty (Lawson 2007; Mooten 2015; Robinson 1997). Whereas cruelty divides and distances through colonial imperative and along racial lines, care seeks relation and proximity. As neoliberal cruelty privatizes and outsources suffering, care acts publicly and reflexively to foment solidarity.

However, in dominant European culture, it has not been care but civility, rationality, fairness and equality that have been privileged in the weighing of morality and justice. These have been bound to the development of the autonomous liberal self, and to men as the prime actors within the public sphere. As these modes of morality have been privileged, feminine ethics have been relegated to the private (Gilligan 1982). So, whereas human morality has been seen to progress through public dialogue, justice and the rules for citizens and governments, private acts of love and responsibility have been dismissed. It is for this reason that civility, rather than care, has been posited as the counterpoint to cruelty because civility corresponds to a set of rules for individuals' moral and public conduct, and to the duties required of citizens in a democracy. So while there is an injunction that modern societies (also liberal ones) should not treat people with cruelty, and should be civil, there has been no particular imperative for care or indeed broad consideration of what that might mean (Robinson 1997).

This is not to say that notions of fairness, equality and redistribution have not resulted in systems we might think of as caring. Indeed they have, and these understandings of care informed the approaches of many international volunteers on Chios. The welfare state in Britain is a good example of a system we think of as caring. But the difference between welfarist and feminist notions of care is that in welfare, care is done *to* you and indeed *to* certain people defined as in need of care: "the infirm, the young/elderly, the dependent, the flawed – ignoring the fact that we, all of us, give and need care" (Lawson 2007, 3). Under Conservative neoliberalism, this categorization of the needy persists, but welfare is argued to cause dependency and so instead of the state, individuals and communities are morally mandated to look after their own and are thereby also made responsible for any failure that follows.

Another system we think of as caring is humanitarianism. In the post-WWII period, this extends welfarism from the national to the international. In so doing, welfarism becomes intertwined with benevolent colonialism often through the figure of the saviour. The saviour identifies a victim (in Chios, the refugee). This victim is seen to be vulnerable, often childlike, and lacking in agency. The saviour (the international volunteer) then takes on the mantle of rescuing the victim, but does so on their own terms, thus enacting the other side of the colonial binary – a fulfilment of maturity, agency and civility (Mutua 2001; Narayan 1995).

These forms of care were evident in Chios but so too were acts of care that were feminist and postcolonial in character. These were less responsibility *for* others (a welfarist, patriarchal and/or colonial model) than responsibility *to* others; they sought not a "bond of continuing dependence" but a "dynamic of interdependence" between supposed strangers (Gilligan 1982, 149). Threaded through welfarism and benevolent colonialism was then a dynamic of interdependence which deconstructed care as the privileged property of the nuclear family and the nation. In these acts, care worked to de-privatize responsibility, and to foster mutuality and solidarity beyond the boundaries of race and nation. In that sense, care on Chios was also located in a wider set of postcolonial and feminist caring relationships of which maids, nannies, nurses, extended communities and solidarity networks have long since been part (Carby 1987; Gunaratnam 2013; Lowe 2015).

This ethics of care did not proceed in accordance with a set of predefined social and moral dispositions but rather was grounded, reflexive and worked out through social practices. As I will discuss below, the depth of reflexive practice was limited, but nonetheless some deconstruction of cultural assumptions, some consideration of an-Other's knowledge, and some attention to the power of the caregiver over the recipients of care, did occur. In this sense, the caring space was also a learning space that unmade and disrupted some of the cruelties that surrounded it (Lawson 2007, 7; Mooten 2015, 8; Spivak 2000; Spivak and Harasym 1990).

Crossings

My partner and I arrived on Chios at the end of January 2016. Our journey, a short flight from Athens, contrasted sharply with the crossings many refugees had already made from the Turkish port of Çeşme. Our quick and comfortable arrival seemed of gross ease compared to the slow and dangerous voyage undertaken by groups of up to seventy people crowded into small rubber dinghies, propelled by five horsepower motors across the winter sea (Figure 1).

That combination of factors was deadly, and after only a few days on the island, more than 200 people had drowned – a small proportion of total sea deaths, a figure estimated to be in the tens of thousands (United Nations 2017). The precarity of life under these conditions made the rhythms of arrival contingent on the weather. When the sea was rough, few boats would come, but when it was calm hundreds of people arrived per day. Carrying terror and relief, they did not stay long. Most moved on after 48 hours, continuing their journey into the freezing Balkans and onto Germany. Among them were Afghans, Iraqis, Syrians; a smaller number of Iranians and Iraqi Kurds; men and women, children and elders. All were cold, wet, tired and hungry.

As the refugees started to arrive in 2015, the Chios Solidarity Collective was formed – a group of left leaning locals collectivized in response to the unfolding situation. This group quickly established an infrastructure of care, collecting clothing donations from local residents, and feeding 200–300 people twice daily – first from an old army canteen (see Figure 2), and then from an improvised kitchen. This nourishment was supplemented by a porridge breakfast, prepared and handed out by a group of Swiss Anarchists who had set up a squat on the port wall. This became a full-time occupation for many of these residents, who would otherwise have been preparing their bars, shops and stalls for the start of the tourist season.

Figure 1. View of the journey across the Aegean from Chios to Çeşme.

Narratives

As they landed on the coast, local narratives and histories shaped the humanity and infrahumanity[3] of refugees. A local wholesaler explained to us how the people of Chios had always welcomed refugees. He was referring to those who came from Turkey to Greece following the 1923 population exchange. The population exchange caused Muslim Greeks to be displaced to Turkey

Figure 2. Army Canteen.

and Turkish Orthodox Greeks to Greece. It created two million refugees dividing the wider region along ethnic and religious lines; 40,000 of these refugees were Anatolian Greeks. They made their way to Chios from Çeşme. Travelling in boats across the Aegean, they took the same journey as refugees today (Hirschon 2003). The wholesaler, like many other of Chios' current 52,000 residents, traced his life through that displacement.

This narrative for care was not only laid down in sea passages and family stories but also in the walls of the city. Once registered by FRONTEX (the EU border force) and the Greek police, men, women and children were asked to move to the main UNHCR camp at Souda. Here the old castle battlements provided a temporary dwelling for hundreds of people, just as it had for Anatolian Greeks 100 years before. In this way, through the sea, personal history and masonry, the wholesaler traced a narrative of care for the new arrivals (Figure 3).

These narratives of care were intertwined with tales of loss in which refugees were also located. In 1881, an earthquake devastated Chios, and this was central to a local narration of tragedy, that also included five centuries of Ottoman dominion; the ethnic cleansing of Orthodox Greeks following the 1923 population exchange; a potential, but yet to materialize, Turkish naval invasion; and, the current "refugee crisis". These stories informed national and racial ideologies, bifurcations of "us" and "them": the Greek civilization overran by barbarians; the Orthodox Greeks slaughtered by Muslim Turks (forgetting similar Greek crimes); and in the context of the "war on terror" (so laden with anti-Muslim and xeno-racisms) the vulnerability of Greek culture to the now alien values of the Islamic East.

Figure 3. UNHCR Souda Camp and Wall.

The coding of loss on these terms was used to make sense of the downward turn in the tourist economy, central to the economic viability of the island. Reeling from Euro-zone austerity programmes and negative media reports on the "refugee crisis", this all-important industry was in decline. But it became the visible presence of migrants on the island and the (much exaggerated) detritus they left on the shore – caused by the shedding of wet clothes and ill-functioning lifejackets – that became the focus for economic concerns.

This racial scapegoating placed out of reach a popular structural analysis of the relationship between hardship in Greece and the wars in central Asia and the Middle East that were displacing millions of people. It hid the ways in which the cruelties of austerity foisted on ordinary Greeks post-2008 financial crisis, were part of the same global configuration of power that forced many refugees from their homes. It further hid the structural racisms that connected the cruelties that ordinary Greeks and refugees shared. The stereotyping of Greeks as lazy and incompetent by central European media legitimized their abandonment, while associating central Europe with integrity and industry. In Syria, Iraq and Afghanistan, anti-Muslim racism reduced human plurality to the sign of the terrorist, permitting killing while inuring the European frontier.

Just as local Greeks mixed narratives for care and cruelty to make sense of the "refugee crisis" so too did international volunteers. These people, mainly from Europe and North America, oriented care through their own histories. Teachers, social workers and environmentalists extended the welfarism they learned at home, to Chios. In so doing, they de-privatized care, returning it to an inter-human relation but at the same time, they adopted paternalistic and colonial stances. As Mooten reminds us, this kind of welfarism is often "a caring relationship ... imbued with domination, responsibility and historical mission" (Mooten 2015, 8).

Many international volunteers had been motivated by the image of Alan Kurdi who died leaving Bodrum, Turkey for Kos, Greece on 2 September 2015. The image of his lifeless frame carried by a Turkish policeman spurred humanitarian sentiment across the West (Papailias 2018). That picture of a male official carrying a child's insensible body created a media framing of security, protection and vulnerability of sufficient magnitude to motivate hundreds of people to leave their daily routines and head to the island. Through these means, dominant tropes of patriarchal care (and its failure) were mobilized as too were racial registers. Kurdi's lighter skin and young age qualified his humanity and victimhood. A few months before, the *Independent* had reported on darker skinned African adults being placed at the bottom of boats so that their optics did not deny them pity when they arrived on Lampedusa (Dearden 2015).

These narratives showed how on Chios, fragments of time were being pieced together to make sense of the unfolding "refugee crisis" – a compendium of re-enactments, not linear stories, whose meeting points provided the basis for general understandings about care but also cruelty. Splintered narratives of negation were gathered to define the contemporary Other (always also a negation of the self). Their telling denied otherwise shared struggles and hid the culpability of the powerful. These cruelties coexisted with narratives of care available through the same history. Here, narratives of care and cruelty intertwined, such that the besieging other was also the childlike victim; the lived memory of loss also the locus of care to Others that suffered loss. Within this, autonomous narratives of care were also evident. Their strands were not of terminal negation but composed from the minor textures of generosity to, and solidarity with, Others. In this way, they persisted as vital resources to local people amid the spiralling, racially designated negativity, providing the vernacular basis for on-going acts of relation and responsibility.

Boat and beaches

Beach rescue, the registration centre and the sharing of food were other sites through which the tensions between care and cruelty on the island could be understood.

Beach rescue on Chios was the principle responsibility of the Cliff Team.[4] The Cliff Team was a group of coast guards and volunteers trained in sea rescue. The Cliff Team placed lookouts at strategic points along the coast and used cars headlights to mark safe landing places. Like lighthouses, these beacons helped incoming boats navigate away from the rocks, and

88

when they reached shallow water, volunteers would wade into the sea from the beach and help people ashore.

Some of this was spectacular. There were tales of endurance. The young men who watched for days and nights at the cliffs edge garnered local fame. Their independence, solitary stationing and motorbikes fed myths of masculinity and heroism. International volunteers' Facebook pages became adorned with images of rescued brown people, heightening the media spectacle and receiving commendations back home. Indeed, it was a truism among many volunteers that you did not really understand the unfolding human plight until you had encountered it in the winter sea.

Yet still, alongside these presentations, many ordinary people risked their lives for people they did not know. Nothing made that verification of humanity starker than the contrasting commandments of FRONTEX and the Greek police. They, in accordance with European Commission directives, categorized the boat people very differently. In response to the efforts of volunteers, these authorities effectively ushered hundreds of people on to the rocks and potentially their deaths by banning the use of car headlights on the coast. They further commanded volunteers and townspeople not to enter the sea to help refugees to land. This was enforced by frequent coastline patrols and by the threat of prosecution under anti-smuggling legislation. When that threat was not a sufficient deterrent, the Commission pushed for an interpretation of European law which meant volunteers could be prosecuted under harsher human trafficking legislation. That contained the perversely ironic charge of cruelty to other humans.

The cruelty of those actions can only be apprehended in a context in which forcibly displaced people were not deemed fully human. Penned in the duplicitous language of human rights, the European Commission's "Draft Council Conclusions on Migrant Smuggling" (Presidency of the Council of the European Union 2016) stipulated the necessity of such action for the regularization and management of refugees, and went so far as to state that it was necessary to improve their lives.

The context for that drafting was New Year's Eve 2016 in Cologne, Germany where news had emerged of recently arrived migrants attacking women during the evening's festivities. The ensuing moral panic had fed extreme-right discourses already gathering after similar reports in Sweden. When Cologne Mayor, Henriette Reker defined the perpetrators as "monstrous" she played the illiberalism and bestial sexuality of migrant men against the feminized white western liberalism they were violating (BBC 2016b).[5] That in turn implied the wider vulnerability of Europe's liberal political body to uncivilized hoards. This was the context in which the "Draft Council Conclusions on Migrant Smuggling" was written. Clinging to liberalism in the midst of authoritarianism, the inflammatory language of monstrosity was replaced in the document with the humanitarian lexicons of help, capacity

RACIAL NATIONALISMS

and management, but the infrahumanity of forcibly displaced people remained, as did the rocks of the Aegean.

The coast of Chios was then a frontier for the development of care and cruelty in Europe. As racist narratives permeated humanitarian legislation and practice, killing was sanctioned at sea through the language of human rights. Contingently, transgressive acts of care were banned. The criminalization of international volunteers aimed to fracture solidarities and facilitate command and rule (Fanon 1991). But here too, care acted autonomously. Although sometimes drawing on welfarist and colonial modes, it was also characterized by collectives of strangers risking their lives for Others. This transgressed individualist and racist designations, and did so when the European border regime was mandating death.

Registration centre

If on the coast the visceral proximity of death to life made clear the struggle between cruelty and care, on the rest of the island the professionalized routines of humanitarianism made these distinctions less easily defined.

Having arrived at the beach, the travellers made a short journey by bus to Tabakika, the registration centre. Established by UNHCR at the end of 2015 and run by the Norwegian Refugee Council, Tabakika was housed in an abandoned leather factory. Patio heaters had been installed and broken windows covered with black plastic to minimize cold draughts. Rest was possible, and the heaters allowed arrivals to dry clothing and sometimes family photos (the few possessions they carried). Although better than the dire and unhealthy conditions of other sites, it was still the bare minimum necessary for human habitation.

Volunteers worked in the "boutique" – a misnamed plywood cubicle in Tabakika that served as a distribution point for donated clothes. It was here that volunteers sorted and then distributed hundreds of items of clothing a day. Coats, head scarves, footwear and undergarments were organized from incoming donations and provided to the refugees. It was here too that volunteers rubbed a small child's feet swollen by cold, and rummaged hopefully through numerous boxes to find the correct size of men's shoes. Here many conversations were held, and milk was given to babies.

Refugees cared for each other. Micro-managed, depoliticized and categorized as items in a logistical flow, displaced people of different nationalities, ethnicities and genders formed bonds of solidarity which mitigated the growing claim on them as "bare life". One Syrian man helped another find footwear. From the Balkans and Germany, information on safe routes was sent and received by mobile phone and shared with others. When a Syrian family was robbed, money was collected and donated from the assembled. In one case, a Syrian woman stood a day and night in the boutique translating clothes requests from the refugees to volunteers. A family she met on route cared for her two children. In this way, refugees and volunteers moved out of their private spheres to act towards each other beyond their designation as nationally and ethically different.

In close proximity to these acts of care were practices of cruelty. The journeys to Chios had not been easy. In addition to losing family at sea, many had fled war and were sharing space with opposing political factions. As Assad supporters passed pictures of men armed with machine guns around, a Syrian man complained. He was being re-traumatized and was asking for care, but the paternalistic and colonial determinant of all refugees as similarly and homogenously vulnerable meant that he was not heard. Among the gathered NGOs, there was no opening for such detailed work.

The mechanisms that did exist focused on the management of the collective body. Tabakika was where the asylum system began. First, refugees queued to register and make their asylum case to FRONTEX and the Greek police. If they could prove they were Syrian or Iranian, they were provisionally accepted for resettlement in central Europe. If not, they were denied, told to cease their journeys and appeal. With many documents lost in war or at sea, and with Afghanis and Iraqis trying understandably to pass as Iranian or Syrian, the process was rather arbitrary – five minutes, a flick of a pen and you had been determined.

This process was managed by numbers and wristbands that were marked to record whether refugees had registered, visited the boutique, received a sleeping bag or foil sheet, and when they were to be processed to the main camp. Posited as politically neutral practices, they were anything but. Through these practices people were reduced from humans, to infrahumans, to categories, for management. On arrival at the registration centre, refugees were offered *either* a sleeping-bag *or* a foil sheet. The choice was recorded on their wristbands. Many opted for the later because it was lighter and easier to travel with. As the night drew in, they realized their mistake. Sleeping bags were better for the low temperatures. When they asked to swap they were turned away. Cold and tired they were left endure a sleepless night at just above zero degrees Celsius. The accountancy system, which designated them not as humans but units in a logistical flow, meant their error was irreversible.

In this way, the registration centre saw racialized boundaries partially deconstructed as people moved beyond their privately, ethnically and nationally defined selves. Here there was kindness, mutuality and degrees of reflection but these were pressed against a machine that categorized and processed with great efficiency and at impressive speed. Marked and assigned to the island's different camps, bonds of care, that need time to develop, were routinely broken. But amid this, there was little animosity between the travellers. They were collectivized in their struggle. They still had hope. The borders

RACIAL NATIONALISMS 91

were open, and a better life lay ahead. Having survived the crossing, the worst was over. Amidst all the negation there was, at that moment, optimism.

Sharing food

Independent of the registration centre's accountancy system was the volunteer-led food infrastructure comprised of the Greek Solidarity Kitchen, the Swiss Anarchist Kitchen and the People's Street Kitchen. My partner and I worked at the People's Street Kitchen.

Food cooked in the People's Street Kitchen was handed out to refugees from the backs of volunteers' cars. Volunteers and recipients understood this not as catering but as sharing food, and as such as an act of care. Time and thought had been invested by volunteers in the preparation of the meals – a process that started the day before with recipes, sourcing ingredients from around the town, preparation of the stock and then on the day chopping and cooking the final ingredients. Unlike the logistics of the registration centre, the sharing of food was a gift that contained more than nutrition. It contained care, and the act of giving generated reciprocity from its recipients, intimated through friendly gesticulations and kind words – hands on hearts, slight embraces and scraps of Farsi, Arabic and English.

These acts threatened the mandate of the Greek police, and as such, they intimidated those involved by banning food distribution from the registration centre and camps. This forced the provision of food to external areas – such as parking areas and access roads – and thereby denied its availability to the elderly, young children, the injured, unwell or disabled – that is to say the most vulnerable people. It also impacted on women who were the main carers of these vulnerable groups. The police deemed these policies necessary to avoid a rat infestation, although no one had seen any rats. Indeed, I would speculate that the police cared little about the proximity of rats to refugees. If they did, it was odd to show that concern by denying cold and hungry people food. More likely was that they mobilized a discourse of hygiene to disrupt the transgressive potential of care.

Other more convoluted disruptions to care were also unfolding. At the beginning of 2016, an NGO called The German Connection arrived on Chios. They brought with them a transit van and festival style kitchen trailer branded with their logo. These vehicles made the distribution of food easier. However, they also altered the exchange, denying the gift and implementing a commercial and capitalized transaction. Although not their intention, the branding of the vehicle, and its industrial capacity turned acts of care from ordinary people into catering by a corporate body. This alienated people from each other, recasting reciprocity as service to a client. Furthermore, the distribution of food from the kitchen trailer elevated the soup servers above the people they were feeding, reducing the possibility for intimacy and introducing a kind of colonial verticality that compounded the benevolence of the act. Sharing food then became catering, and affirmation became dispassion. Hungry refugees were forced into lines, pushing person-to-person to receive food. German Connection volunteers responded spontaneously to this bustle by taking on crowd control roles – donning high-vis vests and assuming the somatic norms of security guards.

These examples highlight the ways in which different forms of giving food corresponded with different possibilities for care and cruelty. Similar to the beaches, the police compounded cruelty by disrupting transgressive acts of solidarity generated by sharing food. The horizontal, informal and interpersonal dimensions of volunteer-led food distribution made it recognizable as a gift that could be reciprocated. It was an exchange not just of food but of care that validated all involved as human. This was in contrast to the actions of The German Connection which through a commercial presentation, vertical spatial arrangement and security practices situated refugees as clients, victims, and unspecified and disorderly masses.

City centre to camp

At the end of January 2016, the Hotspot Programme was announced (European Commission 2016). The programme sought to create a network of refugee accommodation facilities across southern Europe. On Chios, a site called VIAL was the designated location. As volunteers, we were informed that this location was being prepared and that it was being discussed in the town hall. VIAL was subsequently opened, and the transferal of the refugee population from some city centre camps began.

This development drew stark attention to the colonial-spatial dimensions of care and cruelty on the island. Close to the town centre, the original camps ensured new arrivals were folded into everyday urban life, albeit for a few days. They were free to come and go, could purchase goods from local shops, walk in the streets, and stay, if they so wished. This quotidian incorporation made their presence less remarkable and mitigated against the street level racism seen on the neighbouring island of Samos. The civilian geography also provided protection. While the status of "asylum seeker", in the political context sketched above, meant they could not count on the legal protection of any state, they had the protection of the townspeople. Here, while they could be, and were, treated cruelly, they could not be acted towards with impunity.

The Hotspot Programme dismantled this topography of care. On Chios, the proposed hotspot site was on the footprint of an abandoned factory called VIAL, located outside the town and close to the centre of the island. Although refugees were initially free to come and go, the remote location of the site made this difficult. Indeed, that was the point. The relative inaccessibility of the site was justified through the need to reduce racial tensions in the town. However, rather that alleviate xenophobic attitudes, it confirmed by separation that the refugees were dangerous. Negation again fed negation, and the "open" status of the facility quickly became "closed" and fortified; protected and managed by the Greek military under the supervision of the Greek police. At this point, public accountability was cut, and media and volunteers refused access.

The militarization, denial of free movement and the prevention of public oversight gave VIAL historically identifiable characteristics. The people detained there – some of whom had fled war and arbitrary incarceration – equated it with a prison (Smith 2016). But it had more in common with a camp. The facility was not punishing a crime. It was indefinitely containing and controlling a racially depoliticized population in the context of ongoing war through the "temporary and extraordinary measures" invoked by the European Council (2016, 1). Its existence on these terms meant normal provision for human wellbeing was not deemed necessary. There were widespread reports of violence towards its occupants, no water, maggots in the food, and testimony of advanced malnourishment among occupants. This finally resulted in a protest in which the detainees forced the gates back open.

The founding of VIAL demonstrated the ways in which cruelty and care were spatial. Whereas the city, with its accountability, porosity, heterogeneity, everyday custom and movement provided a civilian environment which precluded impunity and facilitated care, the detention centre with its unaccountability, impenetrability, racial exclusivity, security and stasis provided an incubator for excessive cruelty. Formed within the law (not outside it), this was not an arrangement that the contained population consented too. They did not accept their designation on these terms. They refused to abide it.

Conclusion

With the luxury of time not available to refugees or volunteers on Chios that winter, this paper has provided a reflection on, and analysis of, the transgressive potential of care in the context of Europe's prevailing cruelties. The paper shows that cruelty on Chios was deeply rooted in colonial, racial and modern Europe, and that it was unevenly laced through narratives, practices, legislation, bureaucracy and geography. It argues that care was intertwined with cruelty, but also that care was autonomous, distinguishable from, and vital beyond, cruelty's presiding negation.

To explore these dynamics, the essay has been organized as a journey – a format that some will find unconventional but which best addresses the volunteers' and refugees' quotidian and multiple encounters with cruelty and care on the island. The paper takes theory seriously but holds it lightly, foregrounding the narrative of the island and the journeys within it. If readers follow the essay through they will find a story of Chios; a sustained engagement with modernity, colonialism, capitalism and racism; and an analysis of history, narrative, space, bureaucracy, law and social practice informed by feminist and postcolonial thought.

This approach avoids slippage into the kind of over-specialization that hinders appreciation of the multiple and interlocking dimensions of cruelty, and of the plural and transformative capacities of care. It too avoids a parochial analysis, so whilst this is a story of Chios, Chios is not presented as unique or peripheral but central to understanding the current predicaments of Europe.

In more detail, the paper has shown how the expansive and terminal cruelties of Europe, need to be understood in the context of neoliberal social and economic policy, war and fortification; and, how in this context parochial narratives of belonging are established through starker designation of outsiders. This is not a singular formation, but rather one in which local contexts determine the weight of prevailing racist affinities. On Chios, Central European designations of otherness (variously refugees, Muslims, darker skinned people and southern Europeans) find correspondence with the local Other (Turks, Ottomans, Muslims, refugees and the uncivilized).

These narratives are embedded within "extraordinary" European legislation as they are practised in policing, militarization, bureaucracy and security, all of which should be understood as having agency in compounding cruelty, even as they sometimes purport to be for humanitarianism. These forms of cruelty are both banal and excessive; they are found in the registration centre, so that they can be present in the camp. Ultimately, at their various levels, they function to break common bonds of humanity, mutuality and solidarity through appeals to race and fundamental human difference.

As Europe's storm of progress blows sour it is vital that we identify, evaluate and act against these cruelties. Austerity is removing capitalism's myth of meritocracy from those Europeans for which it was made. A dangerous void is opening up and its most available salve comes in tighter racial definition and protection, and a deeper and more virulent refinement of those who must be kept out. This is a damaging and unsustainable pact and one that will only be satiated by more negation and more death.

But rather than develop this argument alone. This essay has also provided a discussion of how, and in what conditions, autonomous acts of care might move beyond the racial and colonial determinants of contemporary Europe. As has been stressed, on Chios, cruelty was too fast and care too fleeting for its transgressive potential to be fully realized, but it was nevertheless evident. Although intertwined and re-signified in cruelty, autonomous strands or care were available and active. This is important, because in contemporary Europe we will not find an ethics of care fully formed, but we can observe its persistence, engaging with it as a living and learning resource. In this way, as we continue to identify what racial modernity is and how it works, we can also know its limits and work towards alterative social arrangements.

To this end, reflection on racial, colonial, patriarchal and modern forms of power; mobilizing narratives of care; seeing yourself in others; refusing consent to negation; becoming responsible to others; organizing horizontally (socially and spatially) on the basis of reciprocity, mutuality and fellow humanity; taking time; and, advocating for heterogeneous social space, are important resources from which we have much to learn. The scope for an ethics of care is wide-reaching and transformative. It has the capacity to remake a mutual society, but it is also painstaking and slow. None of this will stop the cruelty, but care is key to the on-going struggle against it and to the reconsolidation of humanity beyond it.

Notes

1. For more extensive background on European border control and sea-crossings please see (De Genova 2017).
2. This essay draws on my experience as a volunteer on Chios in January 2016 where I worked in the People's Street Kitchen, distributed food to various city centre sites, and sorted and distributed clothing in the registration centre. Some additional material, for example on the development of the Hotspot programme, was collected during a second period of volunteering in the summer of 2017.
3. The designation of humans and infrahumans through racial modernity and colonialism is established in Agamben (1998) and Mbembe (2003).
4. Some names have been changed.
5. As did satirical magazine Charlie Hebdo (BBC 2016a).

Acknowledgements

I would like to sincerely thank the Institute of Race Relations, who gave me the space to publish some initial and formative reflections on care and cruelty in the "refugee crisis" (James 2016). I would also like to thank *darkmatter* editors, the peer reviewers for ERS, Sivamohan Valluvan, Claire Alexander, Ruben Andersson and Victoria Redclift for their generous and detailed comments and feedback on earlier drafts.

Disclosure statement

No potential conflict of interest was reported by the author.

References

Agamben, G. 1998. *Homo Sacer: Sovereign Power and Bare Life*. Stanford, CA: Stanford University Press.

Agier, M. 2011. *Managing the Undesirables: Refugee Camps and Humanitarian Government*. Cambridge: Polity.

Asad, T. 2003. *Formations of the Secular: Christianity, Islam and Modernity*. Stanford, CA: Stanford University Press.

Balibar, E. 2004. *We, the People of Europe? Reflections on Transnational Citizenship*. Princeton, NJ: Princeton University Press.

BBC. 2016a. "Charlie Hebdo Backlash over 'Racist' Alan Kurdi Cartoon." Accessed October 26, 2016. http://www.bbc.co.uk/news/world-europe-35306906.

BBC. 2016b. "Germany Shocked by Cologne New Year Gang Assaults on Women." Accessed September 1, 2016. http://www.bbc.co.uk/news/world-europe-35231046.

Bhabha, H. K. 2008. "On Global Memory: Thoughts on the Barbaric Transmission of Culture." Accessed January 16, 2018. https://www.youtube.com/watch?v = 5Fp6j9Ozpn4.

Carby, H. V. 1987. *Reconstructing Womanhood: The Emergence of the Afro-American Woman Novelist*. Oxford: Oxford University Press.

Cesaire, A. 1972. *Discourse on Colonialism*. New York: Monthly Review Press.

Dearden, L. 2015. "The Darker Your Skin – the Further Down You Go: The Hierarchical System Aboard Italy's Migrant Boats that Governs Who Lives and Who Dies." Accessed November 23, 2016. http://www.independent.co.uk/news/world/europe/the-paler-your-skin-the-higher-up-you-go-the-hierarchical-system-aboard-italys-migrant-boats-that-10193130.html.

De Genova, N. 2017. "Introduction: The Borders of 'Europe' and the European Question." In *The Borders of "Europe": Autonomy of Migration, Tactics of Bordering*, 1–36. Durham: Duke University Press.

European Commission. 2016. *Progress Report on the Implementation of the Hotspots in Greece*. Strasbourg: European Commission.

European Commission. 2018. "Eurostat." Accessed February 2, 2018. http://ec.europa.eu/eurostat/data/database.

European Council. 2016. *EU-Turkey Statement, 18 March 2016*. Brussels: General Secretariat of the Council.

Fanon, F. 1991. *The Wretched of the Earth*. New York: Grove Weidenfeld.

Fassin, D. 2005. "Compassion and Repression: The Moral Economy of Immigration Policies in France." *Cultural Anthropology* 20 (3): 362–387.

Foucault, M. 1977. *Discipline and Punish: The Birth of the Prison*. London: Allen Lane.

Gilligan, C. 1982. *In a Different Voice: Psychological Theory and Women's Development*. Cambridge, MA: Harvard University Press.

Gunaratnam, Y. 2013. *Death and the Migrant: Bodies, Borders and Care*. London: Bloomsbury.

Hirschon, R. 2003. *Crossing the Aegean: An Appraisal of the 1923 Compulsory Population Exchange Between Greece and Turkey*. New York: Berghahn Books.

James, M. 2016. "Care and Cruelty in Chios, Greece." Accessed September 13, 2016. http://www.irr.org.uk/news/cruelty-and-care-in-chios-greece/.

Krugman, P. 2015. "The Case for Cuts Was a Lie. Why Does Britain Still Believe It?" Accessed February 2, 2018. https://www.theguardian.com/business/ng-interactive/2015/apr/29/the-austerity-delusion.

Lawson, V. 2007. "Geographies of Care and Responsibility." *Annals of the Association of American Geographers* 97 (1): 1–11.

Lowe, L. 2015. *The Intimacies of Four Continents*. Durham: Duke.

Mbembe, A. 2003. "Necropolitics." *Public Culture* 15 (1): 11–40.

Montaigne, M.d. (1580) 1993. "On Cruelty." In *Essays*, edited by J. M. Cohen, 174–189. London: Penguin.

Mooten, N. 2015. "Toward a Postcolonial Ethics of Care." *Academia.edu*. Accessed May 26, 2016. http://www.academia.edu/18028845/Toward_a_Postcolonial_Ethics_of_ Care.

Mutua, M. 2001. "Savages, Victims, and Saviours: the Metaphor of Human Rights." *Harvard International Law Journal* 42 (1): 201–245.

Narayan, U. 1995. "Colonialism and Its Others: Considerations on Rights and Care Discourses." *Hypatia* 10 (2): 133–140.

Papailias, P. 2018. "(Un)seeing Dead Refugee Bodies: Mourning Memes, Spectropolitics, and the Haunting of Europe." *Media, Culture & Society*. Accessed January 31, 2019. https://journals.sagepub.com/doi/abs/10.1177/0163443718756178?journalCode= mcsa.

Presidency of the Council of the European Union. 2016. *Draft Council Conclusions on Migrant Smuggling*. Brussels: Coucil of the European Union.

Robinson, F. 1997. "Globalizing Care: Ethics, Feminist Theory, and International Relations." *Alternatives* 22: 113–133.

Schmitt, C. 2008. *The Leviathan in the State Theory of Thomas Hobbes: Meaning and Failure of a Political Symbol*. Chicago, IL: University of Chicago Press.

Smith, H. 2016. "Refugees in Greece Warn of Suicides over EU-Turkey Deal." Accessed September 1, 2016. https://www.theguardian.com/world/2016/apr/07/refugees-in-greece-warn-of-suicides-over-eu-turkey-deal.

Spivak, G. C. 2000. "Claiming Transformation: Travel Notes with Pictures." In *Transformations: Thinking Through Feminism* edited by Sara Ahmed, 119–130. London: Routledge.

Spivak, G. C., and S. Harasym. 1990. *The Post-Colonial Critic: Interviews, Strategies, Dialogues*. London: Routledge.

UNHCR. 2015. "World at War: Global Displacement Trends." UNHCR. Accessed July 6, 2015. http://www.unhcr.org/556725e69.html.

United Nations. 2017. "Mediterranean Crossing Still World's Deadliest for Migrants – UN Report." Accessed April 30, 2018. https://news.un.org/en/story/2017/11/637162-mediterranean-crossing-still-worlds-deadliest-migrants-un-report.

Racism and Brexit: notes towards an antiracist populism

Ben Pitcher

ABSTRACT

This article takes Brexit and Nigel Farage's right-wing populism as a starting point to consider the populist politics of racism and antiracism. I demonstrate how two key figures of right-wing populist discourse – the "white working class" and the "liberal elite" – have come to describe a political grammar with a widespread influence and explanatory resonance across the political spectrum, and which have as a result formed a racial common sense in Brexit Britain. Rather than accept the terms of a debate that has been set by the populist right, I draw on Ernesto Laclau to describe a rival politics of antiracist populism. Although it is far from straightforward to navigate, engagement on the terrain of the popular is not optional if we are to counter a fatalistic tendency to conceive of antiracism as a minority or elite concern.

Populist times

Populism is an important political force in the world today. Political elites in liberal-democratic nation-states are being challenged by a diversity of political actors who attest to represent the will of the people. Donald Trump's claim to champion the interests of "ordinary American people" saw him wrongfooting the mighty party machines of both Democrats and Republicans all the way to the White House. In Europe, populist parties of the left have made significant gains in the aftermath of the European Debt Crisis, Alexis Tsipras's *Syriza* promising to "destroy the oligarchy" and Pablo Iglesias's *Podemos* to depose "La Casta", Spain's political elites (Mason 2015; Tremlett 2015). Right-wing populists, notably Geert Wilders's *Partij voor de Vrijheid* and Marie Le Pen's *Rassemblement national* (the rebooted *Front National*), have moved further into the political mainstream. Britain's vote in June 2016 to leave the European Union is clearly part of this anti-establishment tendency, and Nigel Farage's UKIP played a significant role in cultivating opposition to Britain and Europe's "privileged elite" (Barnes 2016).

This article takes Brexit and Farage's right-wing populism as a starting point to consider the populist politics of racism and antiracism. It takes seriously the idea that the populist moment we are currently experiencing in Britain is not a temporary aberration, and that it is therefore necessary to consider the implications of populism for antiracist practice. Not only do antiracists need to oppose a political climate that feeds racism and xenophobia, they also need to get to grips with how populism has shaped the terms of antiracist struggle. My first objective is to demonstrate how two key figures of right-wing populist discourse – the "white working class" and the "liberal elite" – have come to describe a political grammar with a widespread influence and explanatory resonance across the spectrum of British politics. Exploring the "family resemblances" that connect right-wing populists, the Tories, and sections of the left, I suggest that the opposition between these two figures constitutes a racial common sense in Brexit Britain. To make a break with the political grammar of right-wing populism, I then contend that it is conceptually useful to differentiate between populism's form and its content. Drawing on Ernesto Laclau's theory of populism as a "political logic", I argue that there are theoretically opportunities for the development of an antiracist populism that harnesses popular democratic desire to alternative political ends. Antiracists cannot ignore the rise of populism, and neither can they oppose it without reinforcing the idea that antiracism is itself the project of political elites. While the spectre of racialized nationalism continues to haunt populisms of the left as well as the right, I suggest that antiracist populism is a necessary heuristic to help us understand and act upon a changed terrain of political practice.

The populist racism of the Brexit vote

The first point to acknowledge is the centrality of racism to the Brexit vote. Certainly, there were other factors involved, but Britain's vote to leave Europe was in significant part due to the successful mobilization of anti-immigrant racism by the anti-establishment right. Just as Nigel Farage's infamous "Breaking Point" poster ostensibly named Europe but depicted Syrian refugees in Slovenia, UKIP's injunction to "break free of the EU and take back control of our borders" had a significant and undeniable racial subtext. Never mind the fact that the EU referendum did not remotely address the question of non-European migration, the anti-immigrant vote was, as has long been the case in Britain and across Europe (see Ford 2011), fostered less by antipathy to migrants per se than towards non-white immigrant groups in particular (see Hix, Kaufmann, and Leeper 2017). The visual rhetoric of much of the Brexit campaigning had been preceded by the widespread dissemination of images from the Calais "jungle", having come to prominence in the summer of 2015 as a metonym for the European "refugee crisis" (James 2019), accompanied by tabloid headlines such as the Daily Express's "Send in army to halt migrant invasion" (Reynolds 2015). The evocation of abject black and brown bodies jeopardizing the integrity of Britain's geographical borders was already a mainstay of tabloid media and right-wing political discourse. A conception of migrants as economic and security threats (Virdee and McGeever 2018) had been bolstered by recent government initiatives predicated on "a ratcheting up of anti-migrant feeling" including the "domestication" of border checks in workplaces, hospitals and banks (Jones et al. 2017). Although more "respectable" politicians found it expedient to distance themselves from the UKIP leader – reacting to the "Breaking Point" poster, Tory Brexiteer Boris Johnson responded "That's not my politics and that's not my campaign" (Zeffman 2016) – Farage's influence came to dominate the EU referendum debate. While there was nothing particularly novel about UKIP's anti-immigrant racism per se, what made Farage's appeal distinctive was the way he set himself up against a political establishment. By drawing together an already well-established racist border politics with a forceful critique of political elites (directed both towards Brussels and an acquiescent Westminster), Farage was able to steer Brexit's political coordinates.

Before demonstrating something of the wider political resonances of this splicing together of racism and anti-elitism, I want to first set out in a little more detail the character of Farage's confrontation between people and elite. While not always named directly, two rather more specific figures, set up in opposition to one another and both inflected by race, served to give shape and tone to his populist rhetoric: the "white working class" and the "liberal elite" (see, for example Farage 2018). The white working class are conceived as resistant to (non-white) immigration, while the liberal elite are deaf to their demands; the white working class are culturally conservative and threatened by cultural difference; the liberal elite celebrate and are enriched by multiculturalism. The white working class live in small towns and identify as English or British; the liberal elite live in the metropolis and identify as European and cosmopolitan. The white working class do not censor themselves and speak the truth about race; the liberal elite are transfixed by and seek to impose an agenda of political correctness. This opposition between the white working class and the liberal elite draws on an eclectic range of elements, combining issues of culture and lifestyle together with politics and ideology. Right-wing populists like Farage paint a vivid picture of two irreconcilable groups and the imbalance of power that exists between them: the liberal elite are small in number but large in influence; the white working class are large in number but powerless and disenfranchised. To remedy this inequity, right-wing populists propose a simple and neat solution:

the liberal elite must be deposed and representatives of the people must be installed in power.

It is not hard to unpick the racial politics that is implicit to this framing. When Farage argues that immigration "has left the white working class, effectively, as an underclass" (in Wintour, Watt, and Mason 2014), he uses the language of racial difference to construct a category of identification and victimhood (see Emejulu 2016). In right-wing populist rhetoric, the "white working class" does not only give a name to a group of people, it also implicitly names the cause and agents of their subordination: immigrants and liberal elites. This causality embedded in the "white working class" references a time before its fall, a time apparently before "immigration". It references the long-held but profoundly erroneous fantasy of Britain as a white nation, over which white people have some proprietorial claim (Abbas 2019, Jones 2019). In addition, the figure of the "white working class" refuses an understanding of class that cuts across racial differences. Britain's multicultural working class is hereby fragmented and repackaged so as to prioritize racial difference as a defining element of social conflict. The "white working class" is not, therefore, an innocent empirical description of an existing social group, but a partisan argument about race, proprietorship, entitlement, victimhood and displacement.

We can advance similar kinds of argument about the figure of the "liberal elite", who in right-wing populist discourse are conceived as the relentless champions of immigration and proponents of multicultural diversity. It does not take much critical scrutiny to reveal the fictive nature of this "liberal elite". Even the most laissez-faire of recent UK governments have presided over immigration regimes that have served to both stigmatize economic migrants and exploit their labour. State managers who go out of their way to stress their commitment to oppose racism and discrimination have frequently shown themselves to be apologists for it. Governing elites have certainly learned to speak a "progressive" language of race, but however well intentioned their antiracism is frequently inadequate and self-serving.

By defining political elites by their supposed social liberalism, the discourse of right-wing populism reinforces a false dichotomy in the politics of race. It reproduces a conception of antiracism that is imposed, top down, on a reluctant and prejudiced population. In doing so, it removes from view the hospitable, convivial, "unheralded multiculture" (Gilroy 2004, 108) that has long been part of the fabric of British working class life. Such framings sideline quotidian forms of antiracist politics and solidarity, and write out of the story the central role played in the antiracist struggle by minority communities themselves. Indeed, one of the most notable features of right-wing populists' rhetorical opposition of the figure of the "white working class" to the figure of the "liberal elite" is the virtual absence of anyone who is not racialized as white. While racialized minorities are central to right-wing populist discourse, they exist only to describe the antagonism between both groups. If right-wing populism adapts Orwell's characterization of the nation as a "family with the wrong members in control" (Orwell 1941), then we should also note that it conceives of this family as intrinsically white.

Family resemblances

So much might be considered par for the course from right-wing populists like Farage. What is more remarkable is the extent of right-wing populism's political influence. Consider the rapidity with which the leadership of the Tory Party reframed its stance at their party conference some four months after the Brexit vote. Attempting to put some distance between herself and her predecessor David Cameron – not to mention her own pre-vote association with the Remain campaign – Theresa May spoke of a sense "that many people have today that the world works well for a privileged few, but not for them", and that "too many people in positions of power behave as though they have more in common with international elites than with people down the road". Summarizing this populist affiliation to "the people" against the elite, May insisted that "if you believe you're a citizen of the world, you're a citizen of nowhere". May addressed "the public", who she defined in opposition to politicians and commentators who, she argued, "find your patriotism distasteful, your concerns about immigration parochial, your views about crime illiberal, your attachment to your job security inconvenient." (May 2016; see also Stewart and Walker 2017).

While May's populist turn was evidently an accommodation to the direction of political travel that had been established by UKIP, it is striking to note the extent to which the same variety of political rhetoric – counterposing local publics with "international elites", and returning repeatedly to the theme of immigration and national identity – was adopted across a wide political spectrum as an analysis of the Brexit political conjuncture. Take, for example, the premise that animates David Goodhart's *The Road to Somewhere*, which sets up an opposition between "Somewheres", socially conservative and geographically-bound, and "Anywheres", that cosmopolitan liberal elite (Goodhart 2017). In the analysis of Eric Kaufmann (2017), popular opposition to immigration is a legitimate expression of "racial self-interest" erroneously policed by the antiracist moralism of liberal elites. It became exceedingly common after the Brexit vote for political analysis to share the diagnosis – if not the beliefs – of right-wing populists.

Of particular interest here is the way that the right-wing populist opposition of "white working class" and "liberal elite" have been echoed by some in the Labour party. Consider the response to the Brexit vote by centre-left Labour politician Andy Burnham. While critical of the explicit racism of the far right, Burnham argues that Labour activists need to "take back control of the immigration debate" by listening to and not dismissing "public concerns" out of a fear of "pandering to UKIP". Again, right-wing populists are credited with expressing an authentic popular desire, and Labour activists are framed as thwarted by their own political correctness, left "avoiding people's eyes and shuffling away" (Burnham 2016). If Burnham unintentionally takes for granted the political grammar of right-wing populism, there have been indications that the perceived popular purchase of anti-immigrant positions have at times also inflected the actions of the Labour leadership in its triangulations over Brexit. Jeremy Corbyn's advocacy of a "migrant impact fund" (Corbyn 2016) framed an underfunding problem as a migrant problem, while an abrupt U-turn over Labour's opposition to the 2019 Brexit immigration bill (Stewart 2019) demonstrates ongoing equivocation over the question of free movement.

Other Labour politicians have drawn more explicitly on a racialized discourse, defending the "white working class" against a range of straw targets beloved of right-wing populists: Stephen Kinnock has called for "an end to identity politics" and "obsessing about diversity" in order to "stand up for … the white working class" (Simons 2016), while Angela Raynor has argued that initiatives to tackle gender and race discrimination have "actually had a negative impact on the food chain [for] white working boys" (Nelson 2018). In a recent survey of the racialization of the white working class, Aurélien Mondon and Aaron Winter note how the "white working class" has become "a reactionary proxy for the embodiment of the 'people'" (Mondon and Winter 2018, 2), with analyses highlighting the decline, vulnerability and victimization of the "white working class" increasingly common amongst sections of the British left.[1] Similarly, Malcolm James and Sivamohan Valluvan (2018) take to task a "conflation of essentialised, fetishized whiteness with working-class struggle and anti-capitalism" in left-nationalist arguments around Brexit. Notwithstanding the novel features of the Brexit political conjuncture, there are clear continuities here with a far longer history on the left of "racialized identity politics" (Virdee 2019, 19–21). Some of the key operating assumptions of right-wing populist rhetoric – involving a nativist conception of "the people" and a concern about their displacement by immigrants and minorities – have a long history in the Labour movement and came to be institutionalized in social policy and the British welfare state (see Knowles 1992; Lewis 1996; Paul 1997; Virdee 2014).

There are, to summarize, a range of family resemblances that have allowed right-wing populist rhetoric to resonate right across the political spectrum. Farage's opposition of the "liberal elite" to the "white working class" was part of an exemplary populist manoeuvre that Theresa May's Tories had little choice but to follow, despite the performative contradictions and self-inflicted wounds this entailed for Britain's ruling party. But this populist analysis has had a wider explanatory traction, amongst journalists and commentators, and significantly amongst Labour politicians too. On the face of it, Brexit did highlight an exceedingly stark divide: the National Centre for Social Research counterposes the category of "middle class liberals", who voted 92 per cent remain, with the category of "economically deprived anti-immigration", who voted 95 per cent leave (Swales 2016, 25). Yet these classifications represent extreme fractions of the British population and detract from the fact that the Brexit vote was "disproportionately delivered by the propertied, pensioned, well-off, white *middle class*" (Bhambra 2017, 215). Like other awkward statistics – for example, that three quarters of generally poorer BME voters elected to remain (Begum 2018) – these facts have been sidelined in political commentary and analysis by the simplifications of an engaging story about the white working class, the question of immigration, and the interests of a liberal elite. A very particular story about race has come to dominate in the Brexit political conjuncture, in which certain categories of subject have been given excessively large roles.

The political logic of populism

In the first part of this article I sketched out the political grammar of right-wing populism, acknowledging its influence and explanatory resonance across the spectrum of British politics in the Brexit political conjuncture. In this section, I want to draw on Ernesto Laclau's definition of populism as a "political logic" (Laclau 2005a, 117) as a resource to develop an alternative set of critical perspectives, and to unsettle and render contingent the widely naturalized rhetoric of right-wing populism. Rather than take right-wing populists at their word and accept a fundamental antagonism between the "white working class" and the "liberal elite" over race and immigration, it becomes possible, I suggest, to envisage rival forms of populist politics. An anti-racist response to the rise of right-wing populism in Britain needs to be sceptical of and resistant to taking on understanding of "the people" moulded in the image of the far right: essentially the idea that significant sections of the British people, and particularly the working classes, are intrinsically racist. I will not dispute this interpretation on empirical grounds – it is easy enough to find examples of racism, and easy enough to show how racist hate crime has risen in the Brexit conjuncture, as numerous national and regional figures attest (Corcoran and Smith 2016). Rather I will argue that to get to grips with right-wing populism, antiracism must involve itself in the contestation of the category of "the people". Antiracist populism thus becomes a way of breaking with the political grammar of right-wing populism and its entrenchment in British politics. In making this largely theoretical argument I stop well short of delineating a developed political programme, and I readily acknowledge that the left's nationalist investments that I have sketched above continue to pose some significant challenges to its development. My interest here in rethinking race and populism from first principles is largely heuristic, intended to show how it is important for antiracists to prevent right-wing populists from setting the terms of the debate around race and immigration. To tackle right-wing populism, I will go on to argue, it is necessary to be alert to how populism has come to shape what we what we mean and understand by antiracist practice.

In Laclau's reading populism is not by definition nationalist, racist or anti-immigrant: such characteristics are simply particular to the right-wing populism espoused by the likes of UKIP. Indeed, as far as Laclau is concerned populism does not have any necessary characteristics at all – racism is simply an "ontic" content that can be substituted for an infinite variety of other contents, each (theoretically at least) as contingent as the next. What's significant about populism as a political logic is not its ontic content but its ontological form: an appeal to the popular defines a "frontier of exclusion" between "the people" and their political antagonists (2005a, 81). In Laclau's reading the political logic of populism is therefore constitutive of politics per se. Populism does not describe just the activities of the far right, but that of all actors who seek to determine the trajectory of popular will. In its simplest formulation, populism describes the way in which political identities get established in relation to a constitutive outside (an excluded element which gives political identities shape and meaning by resembling and standing for what they are not). Populism names the process by which differences give way to common cause: the way an otherwise heterogeneous people cohere in the pursuit of a mutual set of interests and against that constitutive outside. To act politically is to play a part in shaping this process, of working to establish these interests as common.[2]

While we may want to look elsewhere to interpret the particular "content" of right-wing populism, the political logic of populism can help us to understand the broader context of its emergence in Brexit Britain. As has been widely recognized in left analysis (see, for example, Mouffe 2005a, 2005b, 2018; Mondon 2013; Yilmaz 2016), mainstream political parties in liberal democratic states have increasingly converged around a neoliberal agenda that has proven to be both depoliticizing and antidemocratic. Managerial elites have made decisions according to market-friendly protocols and precepts that have served to distance them from the terrain of political accountability. Though it is axiomatic in liberal democracies that political parties make some kind of claim to uniqueness in representing the will of the people, neoliberal convergence dampens parties' distinctiveness and places emphasis on their common identity. As elsewhere, the centrist consensus in Britain has precipitated withdrawal from and widespread cynicism towards Westminster politics ("they're all the same"), and it is into this breach that right-wing populists like Nigel Farage have recently stepped. Right-wing populism is, in Chantal Mouffe's analysis, "the consequence of the post-political consensus" (Mouffe 2005b, 51). The fact that the anti-establishment energies unleashed by Farage's UKIP were subsequently drawn upon by Theresa May's establishment Tories is not a contradiction in terms: in accordance with Laclau's reading, the political logic of populism is not the sole preserve of political outsiders, but may be drawn on by anyone capable of making a successful appeal to "the people" (see Pauwels 2014, 184; Moffitt 2016, 47–48).

In noting the significant racist dimension of the Brexit vote, antiracist critique needs to be cautious about accepting without question an inevitable association between racism and populism. The causal logic operative in Farage's argument implies that they are closely correlated (a managerial political elite are deaf to the popular demand to reduce immigration and restore the racial sovereignty of white Britons), but it is conceptually useful here to distinguish between populism's form (its evocation of a people against a political establishment) and its content (its anti-immigrant racism).

I want to do this first to elaborate the possibility that derives, as shown above, from Laclau's theory of populism: there is no necessary relationship between form and content here, and that it would have been possible – if not in these specific political circumstances, then in slightly different ones – to develop a populist appeal to the people against elites grounded in an alternative content (a more progressive iteration might have focused on political elites' capitulation to multinational finance capital, say, or their collusion in the impoverishment of education, healthcare or social security over the last decade of political austerity). I make this theoretical point not in order to claim that alternative populisms would in June 2016 have necessarily been a viable alternative to Brexit's racist nationalism (there is surely little doubt that the racist right had very much the upper hand here). I am merely interested in establishing the possibility of anti-elitist populisms grounded in different content – that it is plausible that a protest might be developed against unresponsive political elites around a different issue, or set of issues. The most cursory reading of political history can furnish any number of examples where this has happened, from the scale of revolutions and anticolonial struggles to that of parish councils: an appeal to the suppressed will of the people is, as Laclau insists, "the political operation *par excellence*" (Laclau 2005a, 153). The democratic inadequacies of Britain's political system mean that the perennial nativist complaint about having "never been asked" about immigration can be easily applied to an infinite range of other topics. At a moment when the political grammar of right-wing populism has such a powerful explanatory grip, Laclau provides an important reminder that popular desire is never given, but always the subject of political contestation.

The idea that populist form might have alternative contents gives us a different way of approaching of the right-wing populism of Brexit. By breaking with the causal association between form and content that right-wing populists set up – that anti-immigrant racism is the suppressed will of the people – it becomes possible to disarticulate one from the other. When anti-immigrant racism is accordingly understood as only one possible content describing this suppressed will, we can begin to think of rival contents to fill out the form of popular desire. Besides the possibility of giving populist form an alternative content, the disarticulation of form and content enables us to consider that part of populism's attraction might in fact relate to its formal qualities. Given that anti-immigrant racism in British politics long precedes the intervention of Farage and UKIP, it follows that we should consider their status as political outsiders as significant to the Brexit political conjuncture.

To put this another way: why should we go along with the fatalistic notion that it is racism that comes first in Brexit's intoxicating blend of racism and populism? Instead, can we not entertain the possibility that Brexit's populist form (the nascent democratic desire to have one's voice heard and taken into account) might have some appeal beyond the particular content (racism) with which it is expressed? I am not trying to suggest that form trumps content and that we can therefore straightforwardly substitute antiracism for racism as if the racist content of Brexit populism was entirely incidental to its appeal. Rather, my argument is that if we can attribute even one small portion of the appeal of Brexit populism to the populist form rather than the racist content – that if even a tiny scrap of the electoral appeal of Brexit was towards an idea of democratic sovereignty and self-determination, expressed in frustration at the neoliberal political consensus – then it becomes possible to reject racism as a fait accompli and pursue a political agenda that seeks to harness the populist form to a rival ("non-racist", or, better, antiracist) content. This is what Mouffe calls the "democratic nucleus" (2018, 22) at the core of populist protest.

Once we have broken with the claimed causal association between the form and content of right-wing populism, we begin to undermine the notion that right-wing populists like Farage are simply giving voice to some intrinsic and heartfelt conviction amongst the people of Britain, as if "tensions around immigration are natural, prepolitical reflexes" (Yilmaz 2016, 6). Rather than adhere to a model of politics that conceives of "the will of the 'people' as something that was constituted *before* representation" (Laclau 2005a, 163–164), Laclau's theory of populism insists that the people and their demand emerge at the same moment. Thus "political practices do not *express* the nature of social agents but, instead, *constitute* the latter" (Laclau 2005b, 33). Political representation is, as Jan-Werner Müller attests, "a dynamic, two-way process, not a matter of reproducing some social and cultural reality that is always already out there" (Müller 2016). In this reading, Brexit racism is not the repressed organic desire of the British people that had just been waiting for a figure like Farage to come along to give it voice. Rather, Brexit racism is in part at least the creation of Farage and his political allies (who are of course not making original arguments but are drawing on long-established reserves of racist nationalism in British political culture). Brexit racism is formed through Farage's appeal to represent the people's will, supported in great part by all those other actors right across the political spectrum and in Britain's news media who take the far right at their word and accept without question the proposition that on some level the British people are intrinsically racist.[3] Such an observation does not mitigate the force of Brexit racism – it is no less racist on account of it being politically confected; its effects are not less real. But it does undermine the causal logic according to which Farage is simply the spokesperson for an already-existing popular desire. The political logic of populism encourages us to recognize the contingency of the relationship between "the people", their political representatives, and the demands that appear to seamlessly join them together in common cause.

By understanding the association between racism and the people as a hegemonic manoeuvre – the establishment of a "common sense" in British politics – it is possible to begin to grasp how disabling this might be to the development of an effective antiracist alternative. The accepted racial common sense of our time suggests that liberal elites have betrayed the will of ordinary socially conservative people, and that the answer to right-wing populism is to give credence to their concerns about immigration as if these emerge, sui generis, without the concerted symbiotic collusion of diverse political actors. This racial common sense gestures towards only two political options: either politicians must listen to and incorporate the people's concerns (the populist option; historically pursued most often by Tory administrations), or they must prevent the expression of popular racism by its containment and distraction (the elitist option; historically pursued most often by Labour administrations). Both of these options have been a mainstay of racial governance since the great populist intervention of Powellism in the late 1960s and early 1970s (see Hall 2017), and while from one perspective they seem to indicate very different kinds of race politics (the appeasement of racism versus the protection of racialized minorities), their shared racial common sense – that the people are racist – describes an underlying conceptual unity. According to the racial common sense that preceded, dominated and succeeded the Brexit vote, antiracist populism is a contradiction in terms: political actors have the option of either listening to, or of suppressing, the racist will of the people.

To question the authenticity of this political diagnosis does not require us to downplay racism's hold in Brexit Britain. Insofar as the abiding racial common sense cultivates and encourages it, racism remains an indisputable fact of national life. And yet it is surely possible to hold at one and the same time to two descriptions of the British people: The first, largely empirical assessment, presents us with a descriptive and critical account of actually-existing racisms, their popular currency, and their embeddedness in the social. The second, largely theoretical assessment, is aimed at the contestation of the terrain of "the people" and does not and cannot for strategic political reasons accept the damning finality that almost invariably accompanies the first. To suggest that there might be a populism that could work to antiracist ends is to delineate an alternative to the racist double-bind of Britain's racial common sense. To be effective, such a populism must reject the self-fulfilling proposition that the people are racist, and begin to construct a popular identity using a different set of assumptions. As I have already indicated, to invest in a notion of "the people" as intrinsically racist is to reinforce a profoundly contestable picture of British society: it is based on a fantasy of white proprietorship, it homogenises Britain's multicultural working class, it exaggerates the antiracism of elites, downplays quotidian forms of antiracist struggle, and renders invisible and voiceless minority communities themselves. By highlighting the contingency of right-wing populism's confident claim to represent the will of "the people" I want to suggest that there are other ways in which "the people" could be imagined and politically mobilized which do not build on a racist kernel. The starting point of antiracist populism would be to seek to fill the populist form with a different kind of content, approaching "the people" as plural, egalitarian, and ethnically diverse.

Criticizing antiracist populism – the problem of nationalism

Critics of this outline of antiracist populism would be absolutely right to point out its largely theoretical and speculative character. Although I have borrowed from the advocates of left populism the idea that neoliberal post-politics is the catalyst of popular desire, I have stopped short of making a direct link between antiracist populism and left populism. I have not set out a political programme for antiracist populism or mapped out the social, political and cultural resources on which it might draw, and nor have I explored the potential for antiracist populism in Jeremy Corbyn's Labour Party. Indeed, my account of the political grammar of right-wing populism has suggested that the explanatory resonances of "liberal elite" versus "white working class" are an ongoing problem in the racial politics of the British left.

My account is and will continue to be in large part a negative one, aimed at demonstrating what antiracism stands to lose by accepting the abiding racial common sense that "the people" are racist. Before I go on to give some specific examples that illustrate why I think antiracists need to contest the terrain of the popular, I want to first deal with the problem of nationalism. However useful Laclau's theory is both to our understanding of the rise of right-wing populism and in illuminating a need to develop antiracism from a different starting point, it has long been subject to criticism from a race perspective. While there is much to learn from Laclau's take on the abstract, formal political logic of populism, there is at times a temptation in its application to selectively foreground or background certain contextual conditions to suit the particular argument that is being made. In Stuart Hall's reading, this is encouraged by a tendency in Laclau (and Mouffe) to "slip from the requirement to recognize the constraints of existing historical formations" (Hall in Grossberg 1996, 148). I note this as a self-criticism of the argument I have been making here: I have readily referenced the concrete conditions and circumstances of a dominant neoliberal political consensus as productive of populist energies, while so far sidestepping full acknowledgement of the unit or units of collective identification that describes "the people" of populist interpellation. We know that far right populists have the fantasy of a white nation to cohere an idea of the people against non-white immigrants, but what equivalent entity might serve an anti-racist populism? It is all very well to gesture towards a diverse and cosmopolitan populism-to-come, but what are the building blocks of such a political community? Without an answer to this question Laclau's contribution is not a theory of politics as such so much as a theory of right-wing populism in particular. Does nationalism denature the very possibility of an antiracist populism?

This is the criticism that was levelled at Laclau by Paul Gilroy back in the early 1980s in his suggestion that, insofar as the nation is implicit to the formation of political identities in Britain, Laclau's conception of the "the people" remains a "racially specific" one (Gilroy 1982, 278). It is a criticism repeated more recently by Benjamin McKean (2016) who similarly argues that hierarchies of race within the nation prevent racialized minorities' identification with a collective political entity, reminding us of the tendency of existing right-wing populisms to be constructed not against powerful elites but less powerful and less wealthy minority and migrant communities. Eric Fassin's critique of left populism in contemporary France is similarly pessimistic about escaping a national and therefore racial subtext in appeals to "the people". Rather than trying to convert voters who identify with right-wing populism it is, Fassin suggests, a better strategy to make a specific political appeal to the left that can potentially resonate with both racialized majorities and minorities (see Fassin et al. 2018). Jean-Luc Mélanchon's left populism has demonstrated that it is in practice very hard to throw out the bathwater of neoliberalism without jeopardizing the baby of cultural diversity.[4]

Such criticisms are entirely valid insofar as we conceive of the Western nation-state as the normative political framework within which "the people" are conceived. If we follow Sadri Khiari in observing that "the notion of people, in its modern sense, was constructed in close connection with the social production of races by colonization" (Khiari 2016, 90), then it is surely the case that Britain's imperial and post-imperial history of racial formation mitigates the possibility of the development of a populism that is not itself striated by racism. Even culturally plural definitions of British national identity depend on the exclusion of racialized outsiders and on racialized hierarchies of belonging (Pitcher 2009). In their reading of Latin American populisms, Cas

RACIAL NATIONALISMS 111

Muddle and Cristóbal Robira Kaltwasser suggest that in relatively poor societies like Mexico, Peru and Venezuela populisms "promote the inclusion of vast groups which are objectively and subjectively excluded from society", but that in relatively affluent societies "the people" tend to be defined in "ethnical" terms (2012, 207). The issue might therefore not be with the theory of populism per se but its application to Western or British politics in particular.

The problem of nationalism certainly is not going to go away for the politics of populism. While Mouffe raises the possibility of escaping nationalist determination in her assertion that what's problematic about populism is not the reference to "the people" but "the way in which this 'people' is constructed" (Mouffe 2005b, 69), her recent work on left populism is somewhat equivocal, advocating as it does strategic engagement with the "strong libidinal investment" in nationalism and patriotism (Mouffe 2018, 71).[5] It is true that one of the great advantages of Laclau's theory is that he understands the social as radically heterogeneous: the constitution of "the people" does not depend on an underlying or pre-existing category of identification like race, nation or class. Yet while can accept in theory that "communities consist of discursive spaces, rather than geographical locations" (Laclau 1990, 245) there remain practical questions about the current political valency of rival deterritorialized conceptions of political community, or of sub-, supra-, or trans-national alternatives to the naturalized territory of race and nation.

A defence of antiracist populism

Although the problem of the racialized nation state is not going to go away for the politics of populism, I want to end this article with a modest defence of antiracist populism. My contention is that the populist moment we are currently experiencing in Britain and beyond is not going to go away any time soon, and that appeals to "the people" against an elite will continue to have a political resonance for some time to come. It is accordingly imperative that we recognize how antiracism fits into all of this. Antiracist populism does not provide an answer or response to the racisms of right-wing populism so much as act as a heuristic to help us understand how the field of antiracist struggle is shaped by our populist moment. It is, in part, out of a need to account for the influence of right-wing populism on antiracism that antiracist populism continues to be an important problem to think through, and with.

The key issue that antiracist populism brings to light is this: antiracism comes down far too often on the wrong side of the distinction between "people" and "elite". In this article's account of the pervasive racial common sense that right-wing populism has consolidated around Brexit, antiracism is constructed as an elite agenda, imposed unwanted on a racist people. When self-identifying "remainers" criticize populist voters as "'unreasonable', 'utopian', 'irrational', 'uneducated', not to say 'stupid'" (De Cleen, Glynos, and Mondon 2018), it is not hard to see how antiracist voices might help to reinforce this formal distinction between people and elite. It is a cleavage that can be deepened, too, by some of the antiracism that takes place on social media – an often righteous policing of words and behaviours by those who know better. This patrician framing has of course long dogged the Labour Party: in 2014, Emily Thornberry tended her resignation from Labour's shadow cabinet after tweeting an image widely interpreted as an insinuation of working-class racism (see Walsh 2014); in the run-up to the 2010 general election, Gordon Brown was castigated for his famous off-camera but inadvertently on-mike assessment of a pensioner complaining about immigration as "just a sort of bigoted woman" (Sky News 2010). Whether such comments are reasonable or justified is besides the point. What matters is their performative affirmation of the distinction between people and elite. Antiracism is hereby framed as a minority concern, characterized by its political correctness, and elaborated as the coalition of threatened minorities and a protective, educated elite.

There are of course significant historical reasons why antiracism has become associated with the political establishment. Civil rights struggles, in the UK and elsewhere, sought legal change to establish anti-discrimination legislation. Racism is recognized in the criminal justice system as a hate crime. While antiracism's institutional struggles are far from complete, there is some latitude to recognize racism in the legal system, and by businesses and schools, and other institutions like the media. These institutional struggles have been very important, but they have helped to reinforce the idea that antiracism is an establishment cause. They help to underpin the notion that antiracism, deriving from a legal injunction or some symbolic figure of top-down authority, watches over the people and passes judgment over their errors.

There are times when right-wing populists have skilfully played on antiracism's legal and institutionalized status in order to reproduce and reinforce the political grammar of right-wing populism. In the summer of 2018 the far right activist known as Tommy Robinson broke court restrictions in the reporting of a sexual abuse trial of a number of predominantly South Asian heritage men accused of grooming underage girls in the English town of Huddersfield (Halliday 2018). Found guilty of contempt of court and jailed for a short period of time, Robinson was able to create a story that not only confirmed his Islamophobic worldview, but which positioned him as the victim of establishment censure. Acting as agent provocateur, Robinson shaped a populist narrative in which a liberal, politically correct elite are shielding the actions of depraved Muslim men from "the people". By censoring Robinson's ability to tell his truth about Islamic culture, the elite's political correctness is revealed to be a betrayal of that people. People and power are

RACIAL NATIONALISMS   113

again represented as on opposing sides over the subject of race. For antiracists to refuse to condemn Robinson as a racist would be morally inadmissible,
but to go ahead and condemn him also plays into his hands, amplifying the
magnitude of his argument and confirming his status as a silenced agent of
the truth.

It is perhaps around the question of neoliberal labour policies that the
unintended consequences of antiracist critique have been most sustained.
Under Labour, Tory and coalition administrations pre-Brexit, the neoliberal
deregulation of the labour market was combined with much public worrying
about the impact of immigration on "public services" and "social cohesion"
(for example, Cabinet Office 2010, 21). In such an atmosphere antiracist
voices rightly defended migrants from anti-immigrant racism, but in doing
so did not always criticize the policies that created the conditions for which
migrants were being blamed. If it is not simultaneously accompanied by
the critique of restricted labour rights, the legitimate defence of free movement can look a lot like the defence of neoliberalism. Antiracism can play
an accidental role in policing the racist side-effects of unchecked neoliberal
governance, and as such can again become marked as an elite discourse.

Antiracist populism, as I have sketched it here, describes a very real need to
understand and engage on a changed terrain of political practice. These brief
examples of the way antiracism has been framed as the project of political
elites indicate some of the challenges antiracism is up against in Brexit's populist political conjuncture. Perhaps above all, they demonstrate that how antiracism works and is understood is not fully under the control of self-
identifying antiracists, but rather is shaped by a range of social actors, including antiracism's antagonists on the populist right. I have tried to show how a
focus on populist form rather than content can prevent antiracists from taking
for granted the naturalized political grammar of right-wing populism, and
begin thinking about alternative appeals to the popular will. While it is far
from straightforward to navigate, engagement on the terrain of the popular
is not optional if we are to counter the fatalistic tendency to render antiracism
as a minority or elite concern.

Notes

1. It is misplaced to read such concerns as a result of the influence of the far right: it
   is possible to trace the figure of the "white working class" in its present incarna-
   tion to the unfolding of communitarian social policy under New Labour (Pitcher
   2009: chapter 3).
2. This article will try to avoid excursus into the detail of Laclau's conceptual universe. My objective here is to draw on the political logic of populism to
   provide a perspective on racism and antiracism in the Brexit conjuncture
   rather than serve as a full elaboration of Laclau's theory. Those interested in a
   bit more detail could take a look at Laclau (2005a, 2005b, 1990, 1996) and

114   RACIAL NATIONALISMS

Laclau and Mouffe (2001). For a recent consideration of how to approach populism as a political logic see De Cleen, Glynos, and Mondon (2018).

3. The role played by the press in a media democracy (see Wodak 2015 § 14.57) is
of course significant in itself. The British media, and particularly the BBC, have
consistently given Farage coverage and airtime disproportionate to UKIP's electoral successes. One obvious explanation of this exposure is that the media have
indeed taken on trust Farage's self-characterization as a "man of the people",
and that this is partly to be understood as the critical failure of a media class
who have accepted their own negative characterization as an out-of-touch
metropolitan elite. Thanks to Gavan Titley for inspiring this last point. See also
Mills (2016).

4. The pressing need for a populist alternative to neoliberalism in France will not
go away. While in 2017 the electorate eventually rallied to neoliberal Macron
against Le Pen, the popular democratic tide on which her party rose remains
unaddressed, and is only likely to amplify further in the years to 2022
however many concessions Macron makes towards the far right.

5. Whether Spanish left populist party Podomos's "patriotic" construction of a ter-
ritorially sovereign people manages to oppose "corporations and banks, not
foreigners and refugees" (Gerbaudo 2017, 56) without racist consequences
remains to be seen.

Disclosure statement

No potential conflict of interest was reported by the author.

ORCID

Ben Pitcher ⓘ http://orcid.org/0000-0002-8071-2643

References

Abbas, Madeline-Sophie. 2019. "Conflating the Muslim Refugee and the Terror Suspect: Responses to the Syrian Refugee Crisis in Brexit Britain." *Ethnic and Racial Studies*, doi:10.1080/01419870.2019.1588339.

Barnes, Joe. 2016. "'If They Try and Stop Us We Will Do It Again!' – Farage Issues Brexit Battle Cry." *Express*, December 8. http://www.express.co.uk/news/uk/741276/nigel-farage-political-elite-blocking-brexit-rant.

Begum, Neema. 2018. "Minority Ethnic Attitudes and the 2016 EU Referendum." http://ukandeu.ac.uk/minority-ethnic-attitudes-and-the-2016-eu-referendum/.

Bhambra, Gurminder K. 2017. "Brexit, Trump, and 'Methodological Whiteness': On the Misrecognition of Race and Class." *The British Journal of Sociology* 68: S214–S232.

Burnham, Andy. 2016. "Labour Needs to Take Back Control of the Immigration Debate", *Guardian*, December 16. https://www.theguardian.com/commentisfree/2016/dec/16/take-back-control-immigration-debate-labour.

Cabinet Office. 2010. *The Coalition: Our Programme for Government*. London: The Cabinet Office.

Corbyn, Jeremy. 2016. "Jeremy Corbyn's Speech to Annual Conference 2016." November 28. https://www.policyforum.labour.org.uk/news/jeremy-corbyn-s-speech-to-annual-conference-2016.

Corcoran, Hannah, and Kevin Smith. 2016. *Hate Crime, England and Wales, 2015-16.* London: Home Office.

De Cleen, Benjamin, Jason Glynos, and Aurélien Mondon. 2018. "Critical Research on Populism: Nine Rules of Engagement." *Organization* 25 (5): 649–661.

Emejulu, Akwugo. 2016. "On the Hideous Whiteness of Brexit." https://www.versobooks.com/blogs/2733-on-the-hideous-whiteness-of-brexit-let-us-be-honest-about-our-past-and-our-present-if-we-truly-seek-to-dismantle-white-supremacy.

Farage, Nigel. 2018. "Nigel Farage On Immigration: The Liberal Elite Still Doesn't Get It!." August 6. https://www.lbc.co.uk/radio/presenters/nigel-farage/nigel-farage-immigration-liberal-elite-doesnt-get/.

Fassin, Éric, Martina Tazzioli, Peter Hallward, and Claudia Aradau. 2018. "Left-Wing Populism." *Radical Philosophy.* https://www.radicalphilosophy.com/article/left-wing-populism.

Ford, Robert. 2011. "Acceptable and Unacceptable Immigrants: How Opposition to Immigration in Britain is Affected by Migrants' Region of Origin." *Journal of Ethnic and Migration Studies* 37 (7): 1017–1037.

Gerbaudo, Paolo. 2017. "The Populist Era." *Soundings* 65: 46–58.

Gilroy, Paul. 1982. "Steppin' Out of Babylon – Race, Class and Autonomy." In Centre for Contemporary Cultural Studies, *The Empire Strikes Back: Race and Racism in 70s Britain.* London: Hutchinson.

Gilroy, Paul. 2004. *After Empire: Melancholia or Convivial Culture.* London: Routledge.

Goodhart, David. 2017. *The Road To Somewhere: The Populist Revolt and the Future of Politics.* London: Hurst and Company.

Grossberg, Lawrence. 1996. "On Postmodernism and Articulation: An Interview with Stuart Hall." In *Stuart Hall: Critical Dialogues in Cultural Studies*, edited by D. Morley, L. Grossberg, and K. H-Chen, 131–150. London: Routledge.

Halliday, Josh. 2018. "How Tommy Robinson Put Huddersfield Grooming Trials at Risk." October 19. https://www.theguardian.com/uk-news/2018/oct/19/how-tommy-robinson-put-huddersfield-grooming-trials-at-risk.

Hall, Stuart. 2017. "Racism and Reaction." In *Stuart Hall: Selected Political Writings.* London: Lawrence and Wishart.

Hix, Simon, Eric Kaufmann, and Thomas J. Leeper. 2017. "UK Voters, Including Leavers, Care More About Reducing Non-EU Than EU Migration." *LSE blog*, May 30. http://blogs.lse.ac.uk/politicsandpolicy/non-eu-migration-is-what-uk-voters-care-most-about/.

James, Malcolm, and Sivamohan Valluvan. 2018. "Left Problems, Nationalism and the Crisis." *Salvage* 6. http://salvage.zone/in-print/left-problems-nationalism-and-the-crisis/.

James, Malcolm. 2019. "Care and cruelty in Chios: the 'refugee crisis' and the limits of Europe." Ethnic and Racial Studies, doi: 10.1080/01419870.2019.1617425.

Jones, Hannah, Yasmin Gunaratnam, Gargi Bhattacharyya, William Davies, Sukhwant Dhaliwal, Kirsten Forkert, Emma Jackson, and Roiyah Saltus. 2017. *Go Home: The Politics of Immigration Controversies.* Manchester: University of Manchester Press.

Jones, Hannah. 2019. "More in Common: The domestication of misogynist white supremacy and the assassination of Jo Cox." *Ethnic and Racial Studies*, doi:10.1080/01419870.2019.1577474.

Kaufmann, Eric. 2017. *"Racial Self-Interest" is not Racism: Ethno-Demographic Interests and the Immigration Debate.* London: Policy Exchange.

Khiari, Sadri. 2016. "The People and the Third People." In *What is a People?*, edited by Alan Badiou, 87–100. New York: Columbia University Press.

Knowles, Caroline. 1992. *Race, Discourse and Labourism.* London: Routledge.

Laclau, Ernesto. 1990. *New Reflections on the Revolution of Our Time*. London: Verso.

Laclau, Ernesto. 1996. *Emancipation(s)*. London: Verso.

Laclau, Ernesto. 2005a. *On Populist Reason*. London: Verso.

Laclau, Ernesto. 2005b. "Populism: What's in a Name?" In *Populism and the Mirror of Democracy*, edited by Francisco Panizza, 32–49. London: Verso.

Laclau, Ernesto, and Chantal Mouffe. 2001. *Hegemony and Socialist Strategy: Towards a Radical Democratic Politics*. 2nd ed. London: Verso.

Lewis, Gail. 1996. "Welfare Settlements and Racialising Practices." *Soundings* 4: 109–119.

Mason, Paul. 2015. "'Hope Begins Today': The Inside Story of Syriza's Rise to Power." *Guardian*, January 28. https://www.theguardian.com/world/2015/jan/28/greek-people-wrote-history-how-syriza-rose-to-power.

May, Theresa. 2016. "Theresa May's Conference Speech in Full." *Telegraph*, October 5. https://www.telegraph.co.uk/news/2016/10/05/theresa-mays-conference-spee ch-in-full/.

McKean, Benjamin L. 2016. "Toward an Inclusive Populism? On the Role of Race and Difference in Laclau's Politics." *Political Theory* 44 (6): 797–820.

Mills, Tom. 2016. *The BBC: Myth of a Public Service*. London: Verso.

Moffitt, Benjamin. 2016. *The Global Rise of Populism: Performance, Political Style and Representation*. Stanford: Stanford University Press.

Mondon, Aurélien. 2013. *The Mainstreaming of the Extreme Right in France and Australia: A Populist Hegemony?*. Farnham, Surrey: Ashgate.

Mondon, Aurélien and Winter, Aaron. 2018. "Whiteness, Populism and the Racialisation of the Working Class in the United Kingdom and the United States", *Identities*. doi:10.1080/1070289X.2018.1552440.

Mouffe, Chantal. 2005a. *On the Political*. London: Routledge.

Mouffe, Chantal. 2005b. "The 'End of Politics' and the Challenge of Right-Wing Populism." In *Populism and the Mirror of Democracy*, edited by Francisco Panizza, 50–71. London: Verso.

Mouffe, Chantal. 2018. *For a Left Populism*. London: Verso.

Muddle, Cas and Cristóbal Robira Kaltwasser. 2012. "Populism: Corrective and Threat to Democracy." In *Populism in Europe and the Americas: Threat of Corrective for Democracy?*, edited by Cas Muddle and Cristóbal Robira Kaltwasser, 205–222. Cambridge: Cambridge University Press.

Müller, Jan-Werner. 2016. "Capitalism in One Family." *London Review of Books* 38 (23): 10–14.

Nelson, Fraser. 2018. "Angela Rayner on Education and White Working-Class Culture." *The Spectator*, January 3. https://blogs.spectator.co.uk/2018/01/angela-rayner-on-education-and-white-working-class-culture/.

Orwell, George. 1941. "The Lion and the Unicorn: Socialism and the English Genius." https://www.orwellfoundation.com/the-orwell-foundation/orwell/essays-and-other-works/the-lion-and-the-unicorn-socialism-and-the-english-genius/.

Paul, Kathleen. 1997. *Whitewashing Britain: Race and Citizenship in the Post-war Era*. New York: Cornell University Press.

Pauwels, Teun. 2014. *Populism in Western Europe*. London: Routledge.

Pitcher, Ben. 2009. *The Politics of Multiculturalism: Race and Racism in Contemporary Britain*. Basingstoke: Palgrave Macmillan.

Reynolds, Mark. 2015. "Send in Army to Halt Migrant Invasion." *Daily Express*. July 30.

Simons, Ned. 2016. "Labour Must Stop 'Obsessing' About Diversity, Says Stephen Kinnock." *Huffington Post*, November 22. https://www.huffingtonpost.co.uk/entry/

labour-must-stop-being-obsessed-with-diversity-says-stephen-kinnock_uk_58342344e4b09025ba335e02?ec_carp=7622205140961093196.

Sky News. 2010. "Brown Makes 'Bigot' Gaffe." *YouTube*, April 28. https://www.youtube.com/watch?v=yEReCN9gO14.

Stewart, Heather. 2019. "Labour Makes Abrupt U-Turn Over Immigration Bill Vote." *Guardian*, January 28. https://www.theguardian.com/politics/2019/jan/28/labour-in-embarrassing-u-turn-over-immigration-bill-vote.

Stewart, Heather and Peter Walker. 2017. "Theresa May Declares War on Brussels, Urging: 'Let Me Fight for Britain'." *Guardian*, May 3. https://www.theguardian.com/politics/2017/may/03/theresa-may-accuses-eu-of-meddling-in-uk-general-election.

Swales, Kirby. 2016. *Understanding the Leave Vote*. London: NatCen Social Research.

Tremlett, Giles. 2015. "The Podemos Revolution: How a Small Group of Radical Academics Changed European Politics." *Guardian*, March 31. https://www.theguardian.com/world/2015/mar/31/podemos-revolution-radical-academics-changed-european-politics.

Virdee, Satnam. 2014. *Race, Class and the Racialized Outsider*. Basingstoke: Palgrave Macmillan.

Virdee, Satnam. 2019. "Racialized Capitalism: An Account of its Contested Origins and Consolidation." *The Sociological Review* 67 (1): 3–27.

Virdee, Satnam and Brendan McGeever. 2018. "Racism, Crisis, Brexit." *Ethnic and Racial Studies* 41: 1802–1819. doi:10.1080/01419870.2017.1361544.

Walsh, James. 2014. "A British Politician Lost Her Job Over a Tweet: How to Explain It To Someone Outside the UK." *Guardian*, November 21. https://www.theguardian.com/politics/2014/nov/21/emily-thornberry-resignation-explain-outside-britain.

Wintour, Patrick, Nicolas Watt, and Rowena Mason. 2014. "Farage v Clegg: Ukip Leader Triumphs in Second Televised Debate." *Guardian*, April 3. https://www.theguardian.com/politics/2014/apr/02/nigel-farage-triumphs-over-nick-clegg-second-debate.

Wodak, Ruth. 2015. *The Politics of Fear: What Right-Wing Discourses Mean*. London: Sage.

Yilmaz, Ferruh. 2016. *How the Workers Became Muslims: Immigration, Culture and Hegemonic Transformation in Europe*. Ann Arbor: University of Michigan Press.

Zeffman, Henry. 2016. "Immoral and Dishonest: MPs from All Sides Lash Out Over Farage Poster." *The Times*, June 17. https://www.thetimes.co.uk/article/immoral-and-dishonest-mps-from-all-sides-lash-out-over-farage-poster-2td870cpk.

"I feel English as fuck": translocality and the performance of alternative identities through rap

Richard Bramwell ⓘ and James Butterworth

ABSTRACT

This article deploys the concept of translocality, in order to move beyond the transnational framework that underpins global hip hop studies. Over the last forty years rap music has become a vibrant and distinctive part of mainstream British life. Through rap young people construct identities that draw upon their local experiences while also connecting them with young people from other localities. These translocal identities affirm a multi-ethnic, urban experience of England in mainstream popular culture. Based on a year of ethnographic research in London and Bristol, we argue that a distinctive rap culture is produced through the performance, production, circulation, and reproduction of rap in and between English cities.

In recent decades there has been a proliferation of scholarly work examining the circulation of rap music around the world. The publication in 2001 of *Global Noise: Rap and Hip Hop Outside the USA*, edited by Tony Mitchell, can be taken as a key marker in the development of the field of hip hop studies. This collection of essays highlighted the burgeoning literature concerned with documenting and analysing "global" hip hop. Whereas, during the 1990s, the emergent field of hip hop studies was characterized by a focus on the USA (Perkins 1996; Rose 1994) the turn of the millennium saw an increasing interest in the trans- and inter-national communicative networks through which this cultural form circulated. The bulk of what has come to be known as global hip hop studies has centred on hip hop in specific local or national contexts outside of the USA and, in many cases, charted the relationship between hip hop in the USA and hip hop in specific "elsewheres" (Condry 2006; Nitzsche and Grünzweig 2013). *Global Noise* and many subsequent publications have also problematized the idea that hip hop is an inherently African-American cultural form, arguing for its value and meaning among a range of marginalized social groups worldwide.

In this context, it is striking how relatively little research has been conducted on rap cultures in the UK. Other than Paul Gilroy's discussions of the role of hip hop in black British (1987, 2004) and black Atlantic (1993) cultures, Hesmondhalgh and Melville's (2001) contribution to *Global Noise*, and Bennett's (1999a) article on rap and white-working-class identities in Newcastle, rap in the UK has been significantly under studied until very recently. The last few years, however, have seen scholars giving British hip hop and grime long overdue attention (Dedman 2011; Bramwell 2015, 2018; White 2016, 2017; Turner 2017). While common narratives pinpoint the USA as the birthplace of hip hop and then track its movement outwards (Mitchell 2001), the history of rap in the UK tells a different story. Although rap cultures in Britain have been influenced by US hip hop in a variety of ways, they have parallel, as opposed to subsequent, histories, developing over several decades with their own debts to a range of Caribbean-derived oral poetic and dance music forms (Johnson 1976; Back 1988; Hesmondhalgh and Melville 2001). Rap in Britain has significantly changed over the last forty years and, since the birth of grime in the early 2000s, rap by English artists has taken a prominent position in the mainstream of British life, while still operating as an important subcultural form. Whether explicitly (Nitzsche and Grünzweig 2013) or implicitly (Bennett 1999a, 1999b), global hip hop studies has privileged a transnational paradigm with the USA as *the* central node in the network. However, we argue that this paradigm is unsuited to the analysis of rap in the UK. Instead, we develop a translocal ethnographic approach through which to examine the grassroots production of rap culture in two English cities, focusing on connections and contingencies *within*, rather than *across*, national boundaries.

Translocality, placed-based identities, and rap cultures

Our analysis of the performance and circulation of rap culture draws on debates around translocality. This concept has been used for some time to examine flows of people and culture. Greiner and Sakdapolrak (2013) identify that scholars from a variety of traditions, including geography, cultural studies and anthropology, have used the term to "describe socio-spatial dynamics and processes of simultaneity and identity formation that transcend boundaries – including, but also extending beyond, those of nation states". Brickell and Datta (2011) highlight that the concept developed out of debates on transnationalism: "the history of translocality itself which has emerged from a concern over the disembedded understanding of transnational networks. Research on translocality primarily refers to how social relationships across locales shape transnational migrant networks, economic exchanges and diasporic space". Although Brickell and Datta's emphasis on migration leads them to focus on transnational movement and networks, Smith (2011) observes "Not all translocal connections are necessarily transnational". Significantly, Appadurai (1996) identifies how, through the use of cultural products circulated by communicative technologies, local subjectivity is produced and nurtured through a "palimpsest of highly local and highly translocal considerations". We deploy translocality to examine how place-based identities are performed in particular locations, how these performances are circulated, and how they are informed by performances in other localities. In this manner we draw on Appadurai's mobilization of translocality to draw attention to the inadequacy of dominant discourses of national belonging to young people's lived experiences and to analyse how these youths produce alternative identifications within the UK.

While a number of scholars have employed translocality to examine hip hop or rap culture, these studies tend to highlight the connections between one particular city or field site and a globalized hip hop culture. This can be seen in Darling-Wolf's analysis of rap in France, which identifies how French rappers are able to adopt a position of resistance, in opposition to American cultural dominance. Although she states that French rap embodies a *banlieue* culture, which is "steeped in experiences of immigration, diaspora, (post)colonialism, and racial struggle", Darling-Wolf (2008) acknowledges that her study neglects to examine the local–local connections within France as well as with other francophone environments. Elafros (2013) uses the term "translocal authentication" in her study of Greek hip hop, to examine how some hip hop practitioners have "sought to legitimate rap as a type of transnational popular culture within the transnational field of cultural production". Elafros (2013) contrasts these practitioners with those who engage in "local authentication" by adopting Greek musical elements in cultural production. This focus on the adaptation of transnational hip hop culture to a "local" context, through the incorporation of elements of national culture, is consistent with the majority of scholarship in the field of global hip hop studies.

Eric Ma's study of Hong Kong bandrooms adopts a translocal focus through which to examine how one particular bandroom, the *a.room*, is connected to other spaces in the city. However, despite his aim of examining "the translocal spatiality of *local/local dynamics*", Ma's (2002) discussion of hip hop culture (through the connections that band members have with American hip hop practitioners and their appearances on Japanese radio stations) returns to a transnational frame. As with Elafros, for Ma a globalized hip hop culture is localized within this new context. By contrast Birgit Englert's (2018) study of popular music in Marseilles draws on the concepts transnationality and translocality, and emphasizes the need to use these related concepts carefully, ensuring "that the two do not become conflated". Englert (2018) uses translocality to examine how Sopranos, a French-Comoran rap artist, prioritizes his *Marseillais* identity over his French identity. Although Englert discusses Sopranos' musical representations of a "cosmopolitan" Marseilles, through the lens of translocality, her focus on one particular artist does not address the mechanisms through which a translocal French rap culture is produced in everyday social life. In this study, we highlight how a distinctive, "UK" rap culture is produced through local performance and translocal dissemination of rap songs. By focusing on grassroots rap culture, we explore how ordinary young people construct translocal subjectivities through the production and use of rap lyrics and music videos.

This article is grounded in a translocal ethnographic approach, involving sustained fieldwork in the St Paul's area of Bristol (South West England) and the areas of Newham and Brixton in London. St Paul's is an inner-city area of Bristol, which from the mid-twentieth century became a home for migrants from Jamaica and other Caribbean islands. Today it is one of the most ethnically diverse parts of the city. The majority of our research in St Paul's centred on Docklands Youth Centre, where dozens of young people from the neighbourhood participated in live rap performance and studio production, the vast majority of whom were black. Brixton in South London and Newham in East London are also ethnically diverse inner-city areas and Brixton, like St Paul's in Bristol, became home to many of the Carribeans who emigrated to Britain following the end of the Second World War. As part of our fieldwork in Newham we visited several youth centres where rap was part of young people's activities to varying degrees. In Brixton, our research took place in a community centre and a youth arts charity, Raw Material, with extensive support and resources for music performance and studio production.

Rap in the UK

As this paper will focus on rap performances in England it is necessary to explain our use of the terms *rap*, *hip hop* and *grime*, particularly as rap and hip hop are often conflated in public discourse. We use the term rap to refer to the practice of lyrical performance, by an MC or rapper, often over an instrumental background (Bennett 1999a; Kajikawa 2015). Our interest in hip hop and grime arises as rap is an important component in both genres of music and the subcultures associated with them. Whereas grime is closely associated with the UK and specifically London, from where it is regarded to have emerged (Dedman 2011; White 2016; Hancox 2018), hip hop is historically linked to the South Bronx (Rose 1994; Chang 2005), and has since become one of the biggest selling global popular music genres. Both hip hop and grime culture are indebted to Jamaican sound system culture and reggae "toasting" (Back 1988; Chang 2005; Bramwell 2015). By focusing our analysis around rap, we wish to cut across musical genres and

122   RACIAL NATIONALISMS

to acknowledge the presence of this cultural practice in Britain prior to the global spread of hip hop in the 1980s and 1990s.

Rap in the UK is indebted to the development of black Atlantic culture (Heathcott 2003) from the mid-twentieth century, which involved transcultural flows between cities such as Kingston in Jamaica, and London and Manchester in the UK. The first Jamaican style sound systems were built in the UK, not long after the arrival of the Jamaican sound system operators in the 1950s (Bradley 2013). With leading figures such as Lloyd Coxsone and Denise Bovell, London's sound systems led to the development of the, distinctively British, Lover's Rock reggae genre, and then, later, jungle music and grime (Bradley 2013). Les Back's (1988) study of sound systems in south east London identifies the similarities between the organization of this black British culture and US hip hop. Back examines how sound systems and "Microphone Chanters" in London differentiated themselves from their Jamaican counterparts through their use of "British Youth Caribbean Creole" and the depiction of everyday life in the UK. Both Back (1988) and Hesmondhalgh and Melville (2001) identify how pre-existing British Caribbean cultural practices facilitated the adoption and popularization of hip hop music in Britain.

UK hip hop emerged as a vibrant and distinctive scene during the late 1980s and early 1990s, with MCs such as Rebel MC, Black Twang, and the London Posse, drawing overtly on US hip hop styles while also incorporating influences from England and the Caribbean. Alongside the emergence of this scene, the development of jungle (Bradley 2013) and the crossover success of "Incredible" by M-Beat with General Levy in 1994 (Noys 1995), reveal a continuing identification with the Caribbean within black British culture. At the beginning of the new millennium a significant shift occurred in British rap culture, with the emergence of grime. A generation of MCs that had grown up immersed in reggae culture (including Wiley and other members of the Pay As You Go Cartel) emerged through the structures of the UK Garage scene, producing a distinctively new sound (Bramwell 2015). "Reggae suffused the general atmosphere that the grime generation grew up in, tracing direct ancestral links from Britain's pre-acid house reggae culture, some of it imported from the Caribbean, some of it created by black Britons" (Hancox 2018). In 2003 Dizzee Rascal was awarded the Mercury Music Prize for his album *Boy In Da Corner*. Since then, grime's rise – and the string of top ten singles that accompanied it – has made an important contribution to the mainstreaming of black culture in the UK.

More recently drill, which developed out of the trap music genre in Chicago (Thapar 2017), has risen to prominence in Britain. In contrast to grime's association with east London, "UK drill" is popularly associated with sites in south London, including Brixton and Tulse Hill, although it has spread much more widely. The lyrics of this rap genre are marked by territorial claims, affirmations of gang affiliation, and frequent acts of violence. The popularity of this genre and associations made between the music and rising knife crime in London, have led to increasing surveillance of music videos by the police and youth offending teams (White 2017). While we use the term rap to refer to the verbal practice of rapping, which cuts across musical genres, the young people we spoke with had a keen understanding of generic distinctions and made conscious decisions about the genres they would employ in their creative practice.

Over the course of this paper we explore how, through the performance of rap lyrics and the circulation of rap culture, English youths represent their experiences and identifications, sharing these with other young people in cities across the country. We highlight the role that digital communications play in the processes of production, dissemination and consumption. Young people use these communicative technologies to give shape and meaning to an alternative mode of life in England. In contrast to pervasive nostalgia around Englishness as rural idyll, this alternative mode of life is very much set in the present, it is future oriented, and it is urban.

Place and race in rap performance

In his critique of cultural studies, Arjun Appadurai (1996) raises the question of the type of ethnographic practice appropriate to the examination of translocalities. We draw on multi-sited ethnographies of urban youth culture (Bramwell 2015; James 2015). However, we have broadened our focus beyond the limits of the city or the borough, in order to work towards the development of a translocal ethnographic practice. This study of the performance of identity through rap was conducted as part of a larger study of rap culture within a variety of state-funded institutions in England. Like previous studies of rap culture in the UK (Bramwell 2015; White 2016; Turner 2017) we employed semi-structured interviews and participant observation and, additionally, used a video recorder in order to capture rap in performance as an embodied, ephemeral and social practice. We conducted more than twenty interviews with young adults and youth workers in youth centres, a community centre and an arts charity, spanning sites in London and Bristol. We also engaged in numerous informal conversations with youths under the age of sixteen. Interviews lasted on average one hour and twenty minutes, with longer interviews (of up to three hours) conducted over two or three sessions. All interviews were recorded on a dictaphone, with the consent of those participating. Interviewees were given the option to *not* remain anonymous so that they could be credited for their ideas on rap culture (Elafros 2013). Our routes into the various organizational settings in which we worked were through managers, who introduced us to staff and young people. Interviews were conducted either in these institutional settings or nearby in the local area. We observed hundreds of rap performances – from the staged to the spontaneous – by research participants in the arts charity, community centre and youth centres, as well as outside them, over the course of one year of fieldwork.

Spirits are high in the studio on a warm Friday evening in May. It's Billy's birthday and a group of five MCs are gathered together with Latoya, a producer, in one of the recording studios at Raw Material, a youth arts charity in Stockwell, south London. Billy, holding a microphone in his hand, stands opposite Armani, as the others look on. As part of a freestyle battle, he gestures towards and points at his opponent as he raps his lyrics into the mic: "Call me the white man, call me a Richardson. Where the fuck I come from, I come from Brixton!". As he continues, Billy undermines Armani first by attacking his opponent's lyrics, then by claiming sexual relations with the rapper's girlfriend, and finally by questioning Armani's integrity: "What are we saying, cause those bars ain't really righteous. What are we saying, cause I saw you going to pick up the glock, cuz. … What are we saying done know I just fucked your bitch. Anyway, done know I heard that you're a snitch". At one point Billy's friend and collaborator, Ishaaq, places his arm around him and chimes in with the invective Billy directs at his antagonist. In the same moment Armani raises his fist to be touched by Billy's. The audience respond to the performance with laughter, before Ishaaq takes the microphone and repeats the phrase "little nigger, run and hide" while gesturing with his hand towards Armani. The event is imbued with humour and Armani laughs at some of the most cutting remarks.

Billy's performance deploys a variety of references through which this young, white, working-class man constructs his persona, Billski. In particular the defensive statements "call me the white man, call me a Richardson", which highlight Billy's racial identity and then associate it with infamous members of south London's organized crime world, are followed by a declaration of the rapper's claim to a location strongly associated with black British cultural production and political activism ("where the fuck I come from, I come from Brixton"). In this manner, Billski prioritizes place over race in the construction of his identity. Brixton's ethnic and cultural associations play an important role in this conjuring of identity. Billy (who lives nearby in Stockwell) solicits identification from members of the audience, who acknowledge his claim to "come from Brixton" and appreciate the cultural significance of this topos.

Murray Forman (2000) argues that in rap music "space and race figure prominently as organising concepts implicated in the delineation of a vast range of fictional or actually existing social practices". In this event, we also see how these concepts are invoked through performance and used to solicit identification and produce a collective identity. Gilroy's emphasis on the practical activity through which black identity is produced is useful in considering how race, space and place are used to conjure Billski's persona in this performance: "Though this identity is often felt to be natural and spontaneous, it remains the outcome of practical activity: language, gesture, bodily significa-tion, desires" (Gilroy 1991, 127). The performance is structured and unfolds through oral exchange, physical gestures and bodily contact between Billy and Armani as well as between the two central performers and the others present. Significantly, with the exception of Billy, all the participants in this event are either black British African or black British Caribbean. Billski is brought into social being through a combination of linguistic skill, references to race and place, bodily gestures, and the audience's affirmation of Billy's belonging to a multi-ethnic community.

It is also important to note that, not only do race and space figure within the performance, but the performance takes place in an institutional setting: a youth arts charity. This institution, Raw Material, facilitates partici-pation in rap culture, in a similar manner to the "alternative spaces of culture" discussed by Hoyler and Mager (2005) in relation to German youth and community centres. Prior to rapping his response to Billy, Armani repeats the phrase "that's alright", over the audience's laughter, before a brief exchange between the pair:

Armani	that's alright … Billski, because we look up to you anyway, yeah. Champion, you get me? Once a King, always a King, you see me? I'm not really much of a freestyler anyway. Let's see what we got here.
Billy	You asked for it
Armani	Yeah I know, I did! 'cause that's the only way you get better.

The exchange highlights how this performance constitutes part of an informal learning process. Both Billy and Armani are engaged in the demonstration and development of their craft. Furthermore, the members of the group assembled in this space are all participating in the construction of identity through their practical activity. Significantly the Billski persona is performed through an identification with a place long associated with black popular culture, as well as the simultaneous invocation and dismissal of racial differ-ence. This identity is affirmed through the physical and oral participation of the audience in this performance. While humour plays a significant role in affirming this identity, it is important to note that it is grounded through a rhetorical invocation of place, and Brixton's distinctive ethnoscape.

Translocality and the "UK" rap scene

The importance of local identity to rap culture has been evident in our fieldwork in both London and Bristol. This emerges through written lyrics, bodily gestures and speech acts as well as through social relations and the use of cultural products. However, identification with the local often operates alongside a corresponding emphasis on the translocal, as rappers reference, listen to, connect themselves with, and distinguish themselves from, the locals of other English cities. While geographers have long used the concept of translocality to analyse cultural and migratory flows (Brickell and Datta 2011), it has most often been deployed in the examination of connections across or outside of national boundaries (Greiner and Sakdapolrak 2013). As a result of our focus on rappers' representations of contemporary urban dwelling, we wish to highlight that alongside the construction of identifications beyond the limits of the national (Ma 2002; Elafros 2013), translocality might be fruitfully employed in the examination of connections within the nation (Englert 2018) and deployed in understanding how the nation itself is (re)imagined.

In addition to constructing their identities through lyrical references to their locality, aspiring rappers' use of rap music and videos draws attention to the translocal networks through which rap culture is formed. On several occasions we encountered boys at the Docklands Youth Centre, in St Paul's, Bristol, watching music videos made by other young people in Bristol and beyond, which had been uploaded to YouTube. The Docklands boys would collectively view and discuss these videos. A large number of these were shot in and around Brixton, in London. In particular, the 67 crew, who hailed from Brixton, were well known amongst the boys at Docklands through these videos. We observed one of the Docklands boys making his own recording in the studio, drawing on lyrics from a 67 video. While London was clearly an important city in the imagination of aspiring artists at the youth centre, specific parts of the capital had a special resonance for these youths and young adults in the St Paul's area of Bristol. All but a couple of the dozens of boys we observed in the studio at Docklands over six months were black, and Brixton – as a hub of black British cultural production – was a key node in the public to which they were oriented.

We have touched upon the significance of Brixton in our discussion of the construction of Billy's "Billski" persona, above. However, what we want to emphasize here is how rap culture is constructed through the performance of rap lyrics *and* the circulation of rap music videos via social media. Through the performance, dissemination, consumption and reuse of rap lyrics, young people develop translocal subjectivities. Significantly the vast majority of YouTube videos viewed by the boys at Docklands featured boys from either Bristol or other English cities (i.e. not from the rest of the rest of the UK, nor from the USA). Here, translocality can be used to understand how a distinctive, grassroots, rap culture is produced through a network of exchange, that privileges neighbourhoods in English towns and cities with large working-class and ethnic minority populations.

The interplay between the local and the translocal is apparent in the self-description of Stripzz, a seventeen-year-old rapper from Bristol. During our fieldwork, Stripzz regularly attended Docklands youth centre. He had recorded several songs and performed as part of the collective Oosowavey, which had formed at the youth centre. This aspiring artist's explanation of the importance of representing his city, deploys references to the UK, Bristol and other English cities:

> I'm a UK guy, wanna represent UK, do you know what I mean? ... this is where I'm from. And it's not even specifically UK, it's mainly Bristol. Bristol's an under-ated city, the music scene here is amazing. ... London, it's the capital and every-one is straight to London but I believe Bristol, we're just as good as London.

Like his contemporaries at Docklands youth centre, Stripzz regularly mentions Bristol in his lyrics and makes shout outs to other Bristol rappers. Just as the Bristol scene is discursively constituted through the production and circula-tion of these rap songs, an English rap culture emerges through a network of urban centres that operate as symbolic as well as physical locations of cul-tural production. Stripzz spoke of taking inspiration from the Birmingham rapper, Lady Leshurr, as well as Bugzy Malone from Manchester, and saw a kind of equivalence between these artists and himself: "I respect them because they are doing their thing for their city. They're doing what I- what we're all trying to do really". Rap culture is thriving in a range of urban centres in England – including Bristol, Birmingham, Nottingham and Manche-ster to name but a few. However, London is clearly an important junction point. London's prominence is evident both in terms of the sheer scale of cul-tural and economic activity surrounding rap in the capital as well as the sym-bolic power of London rap culture.

The grime scene is strongly associated with London, in general, and Bow in east London in particular (Bramwell 2015). However, other parts of capital, such as Brixton (which is associated particularly with UK drill and the "road rap" genre that preceded it), also continue to play a significant role in structur-ing understandings of "UK" rap culture. What is striking is that despite the rhetoric of "UK" or "British" rap by Stripzz and others, locations in Scotland, Wales and Northern Ireland are rarely (if ever) mentioned by rappers from cities in England. Even in Bristol, we have not once encountered Welsh people or places being referenced in relation to rap culture, despite the Welsh border being less than 20 miles away and Cardiff, the Welsh capital city, just over 40 miles away. By contrast, references to rappers and rap scenes in English cities like nearby Gloucester as well as Birmingham, Notting-ham and Manchester are relatively common. We argue that through the per-formance of rap lyrics in cities across England, and the circulation of rappers' representations of themselves, their neighbourhoods, and their cities in music videos, a distinctive "UK" rap culture is imagined, performed, and practised in young people's everyday lives, through a network of translocal cultural flow that privileges urban centres in England. Although grime culture is present in Cardiff and Glasgow, the rap scenes in these cities are obscured by the pro-minence of these translocal English networks that make up "UK" rap culture.

Negotiating territory, performing translocality

One Wednesday evening in spring 2016, we arrived at the studio in Docklands, Bristol, and walked in on a noticeably tense atmosphere and a serious conversation taking place between a few young people and Duppy, Hans and Cherelle, the team of adults that run the studio. It transpired that Stripzz's crew had become the subject of "beef" from another crew circulated online through a music video. The offending crew had shot a video in the neighbourhood of a rival group, and in the course of their track rapped the line "them man don't want smoke, they're like Oosowavey". For the Oosowavey boys, this had been an unprovoked attack, drawing them into a kind of territorial conflict that they did not want to be involved with. Noticeably affected by the situation, Stripzz, was keen to push back and saw the recording booth as a place to do it. However, this was not to be a tit-for-tat exchange but an attempt to take the higher ground by focusing on his "own thing". He had arranged to record a collaboration that night with Murkzy, another young rapper he had been communicating with on Facebook Messenger. Murkzy delivered his contribution to the track first, and he was immediately followed into the booth by Stripzz, with staff-member Cherelle recording the track and acting as their producer. Reading from a sheet of A4 paper, Stripzz delivered his lines into the mic, gesturing with his right hand as he rapped. Stripzz's verse referred to both Bristol and the South West, but his declaration that he is "reppin' Bris' not Endz" [representing the whole city, not just his neighbourhood] conveys a desire to project himself beyond the territorial disputes of local groups. The song ends with the lines "Beef I just lef' it. I'm here for the grind no question./ My young G's show progression. Hater's that I'm your obsession". When he emerged from the booth, Stripzz was both energized and very pleased with his performance. We asked what the track was called and, after briefly conferring, they agreed "Shook".

Less than three weeks later a full music video for "Shook" had been shot and posted on SimzCityTV, the same YouTube channel as the video that had prompted Stripzz's response. In that video the crew that insult Oosowavey – drawing on the conventions of the drill genre – walk down a high-street, point to the sign of a local pub, and clearly identify their ability to occupy local territory. By contrast, the music video for "Shook" depicts Stripzz and Murkzy standing in and walking through Bristol's streets and a local housing estate. "Shook" is shot during the daytime and, although various vehicles enter the frame, there are no images of street signs. While the video is clearly set in a residential area, there is no attempt to identify this particular locale within the city. This music video is tightly focused on the performance of the two rappers, and the chorus emphasizes their social orientation:

> Mum told me not every single person you meet is good
> Don't matter where they come from, from the rich parts or from the "hood
> So I'm gonna stay in my lane, man can't take me for a mook

Don't care who you are, don't care where you're from
Go and let another man go and think I'm shook".

The representation of a resilient masculinity in this music video is constructed through a particular orientation to locality: "reppin' Bris' not Ends". The song's emphasis on resisting "beef", its disavowal of territorial allegiance, the affirmation of a maternal moral figure, and the MCs' prioritization of personal development, contributes to a struggle over the shape and meaning of contemporary urban dwelling and citizenship. Rather than seeing representations of the "neighbourhood" solely as part of a generic formula, "Shook" is better understood as a response to another video. Therefore this representation is part of a cultural debate about the scale on which black urban life should be lived, and the role of one's locality in shaping identity.

Importantly, for Stripzz, his representation of himself on Bristol's streets is not solely a representation of his city but also a representation of the nation:

> It's like Stormzy, he's obviously backing London because he's from London, but then he's repping the whole of the UK, because he's from the UK, right? So I'm repping Bristol, but then obviously Bristol is the UK, so I'm repping UK as well. But there's no UK or Bristol, it's just both equally.

This imagined connection between specific cities, through which representations of the "whole of the UK" are produced, highlights the importance of a particular form of translocality in English rap culture. The performance of rap songs and the circulation of videos by artists and crews such as Billy, Stripzz and Murkzy contributes to an alternate public sphere through grassroots rap culture. In *After Empire*, Paul Gilroy (2004) highlights how songs, by figures such as Mike Skinner, have a "precious ability to transport English ethnicity into the present". We want to build on this observation and suggest that the communicative technologies that connect London's black public sphere (Baker 1996; Bramwell 2015) to those of other urban centres, have facilitated a reimagining of national identity that is meaningful to ordinary young people.

Reimagining Englishness

We argue that rap is a medium through which alternative English identities are performed. In our research on rap culture in England we have encountered a wide range of national and ethnic subject positions, ranging from deep affirmations of Englishness through to bold negations of (hegemonic) English identity. These various subject positions are constructed through an engagement with a network of black cultural production and consumption that links various urban centres in England and from which emerges a rap culture that is widely conceived and experienced as distinctly "UK". Notably, "UK" in this context often operates as an unconscious euphemism for

England. We argue that a generation of youths actively construct identities and feel intimately connected to an English rap culture, even while many of those youths might disavow or be ambivalent towards Englishness writ large.

Talk about English identity and governance has gained increasing prominence in public consciousness and political discourse in recent years. This is due, in large part, to devolution processes that have transferred legislative power from the UK Parliament to the newly founded Scottish Parliament (1999) and National Assembly for Wales (1998). Meanwhile, England has continued to be wholly governed by the UK Parliament. This situation has fortified Scottish and, to a lesser extent, Welsh, nationalism, leaving English identity and politics in a state of confusion and uncertainty. That uncertainty has been intensified through debates during and after the referendum on Scottish independence in 2014 and the European Union membership referendum in 2016. Since the mid-twentieth century, English nationalism developed as a relatively niche political project of the Right. Figures such as John Major (1993) and Roger Scruton (2016) have attempted to construct notions of England and Englishness, typically by drawing on mythical images of a tranquil rural or suburban past. These attempts to stabilize a spectral Englishness, fortify their fragile but hegemonic images by conjuring notions of a deep historical continuity (Anderson 1991) of an ethnically homogeneous national community.

Recently, figures on the Left, such as the former Labour Government Minister, John Denham, and the Labour MP, Tristram Hunt, have made the case for the Left to embrace and help shape a distinctly English identity and politics. In 2016, prior to the European Union membership referendum, Hunt argued that "the Labour Party has not been explicit enough about its love of the country" in a "contemporary Europe where the politics of national identity demand whole new levels of confidence when it comes to defending the national interest". While we agree that English identity must be the subject of renewed political debate, we find it necessary to highlight that even in Hunt's appeal to embrace English identity his references to "the wild England of peaks and lakes; the historic England of country houses, minsters and castles" conjure notions of an England inhabited by relatively few today. It is important to highlight that the opening up of Britishness to blacks and Asians was the result of sustained cultural, political and scholarly work (Hall 1995). We suggest that for politicians to play a role in shaping the forms and values that define England, in a manner that is relevant to the experiences of those that they seek to represent, greater engagement with how English identity is constructed through the nation's popular cultures is required. Furthermore, we argue that as one of the most popular musical genres in the UK, rap music provides an important portal through which to examine how young people in England represent themselves and develop a sense of national belonging that is distinct from that promoted by either the political Right or Left. This cultural and political work is made all the more necessary in the context of Brexit, where the aims of the UK government often operate in sharp divergence to the varied interests and ambitions of the UK's constituent nations.

Chilli, whose mother is from Newcastle and father from Pakistan, grew up in east London and feels a strong sense of Englishness:

> I feel English as fuck … I definitely feel English, like now obviously I know my roots now, and like I'm half Pakistani, half English. But I was brought up English and my dad wasn't about, so I was brought up with my mum around Upton Park, like proper East London Cockney kind of shit. Like caf' in the morning, and all of that malarkey.

Chilli's representation of Englishness is constructed not only through reference to his mother's national identity, but also to particular forms of language and sociality. Chilli first came to participate in hip hop and grime cultures through school and is now a full-time dancer, specializing in breakdance. Despite growing up within the context of the emerging grime scene, he exercised a choice over the kind of rap culture in which he participated.

> When I was in secondary school grime played a big part in it, and everyone was spitting bars, so everyone was spraying. I wasn't really – I was into it, but I never did it myself. But it was only until after I got into hip hop, and it wasn't so much the grime that influenced me, it was more so the hip hop. … Now, if I spit, I will spit grime more so to hip hop.

Alongside his informal learning and participation in rap culture in the playground, Chilli's school also provided him with his first opportunity to engage with breakdance.

> I started as like just doing dance at my school, and I was learning breakdancing on the side. And then as I was kind of getting into it and I was starting to learn more, I just ended up taking the B-boy route.

Although his early interests in rap culture were developed through hip hop, in preference to grime, Chilli's current inclination towards grime draws on notions of the authenticity and social relevance of rap from the UK, in comparison to US hip hop.

> I think I just listen to better UK music, but it's just like you can relate to it. With American music it's all cool, whereas it's just like super swaggy or just super like gang-bangy. But with UK it's like just makes more sense to me, innit, really? It's like it's not so gang-bangy, but the slang is the same, the situation is the same.

These contrasting orientations, towards both the USA and the UK, highlight the issues present in attempting to think critically about black cultural traditions and the role that rap plays in identity formation. Here, the question

132 RACIAL NATIONALISMS

of origins is put into abeyance, while rap's relevance to social circumstances and lived experience is brought to the fore.

Furthermore, Billy and Chilli's participation in rap performances reveal how the interests and identifications that are shared by the denizens of these urban spaces are explored through this cultural form (denizens who of course boast a complex array of racial and ethnic backgrounds). This coincides with Monique Charles' notion of the "grime generation", held together by what she describes as "cross-race working-class identities" (Charles 2018). While Charles' frame of reference centres on London we want to highlight how such identities operate beyond the capital, translocally, in and between ethnically diverse working-class urban centres in England and, in turn, provoking a reimagination of an English public, from the ground up.

This public, which is given shape by the performance and circulation of rap culture, points to an emergent sense of national belonging that is largely unrecognized by the political mainstream. However, the engagement with grime artists by the Labour Party leader Jeremy Corbyn in the run up to the 2017 UK General Election and the corresponding rallying of the "Grime4Corbyn" movement presents us with an exception. Jones (2018) argues that under the leadership of Jeremy Corbyn the Labour Party was more willing to engage with youth issues, which "played an important part in the upswing in turnout and political engagement by young people in 2017". In turn, a number of "organic intellectuals" within the grime scene came out in support of Corbyn (Charles 2018). We suggest that the coincidence of Corbynite politics and grime has to do, in large part, with Corbyn's upturning of the status quo, leading to a reimagination of national belonging via the prism of social justice in a way that privileges urban, ethnically diverse and working-class subjectivies. While we have observed a strong orientation towards collaborative practices and concern with urban life in rap culture, what also emerges from our translocal ethnography is a significant emphasis on forms of belonging, social justice, and collective self-improvement. We argue that a more sustained engagement with the experiences and practices of these urban youths is required by political leaders. Through such sustained engagement it may be possible to foster the nascent sense of national identity that we have observed, which is grounded in lived (trans)local experience and therefore meaningful and relevant to contemporary England's multi-ethnic citizenry.

Conclusion

In this article we have attempted to move beyond the transnational framework that underpins global hip hop studies. Through the development of a translocal ethnography, we have examined how young people perform place-based identities through rap. By focusing on grassroots rap culture we have been able to identify how young people construct translocal subjectivities through the production, dissemination and use of rap lyrics and music video. Although this translocal ethnography is unable to develop the deep engagement with a single, geographically bounded, community, possible through traditional ethnographic practice, it opens possibilities for understanding processes through which young people's highly translocal and highly local subjectivities are constructed. Place-based identities are not only produced through rhetorical invocations of place, but also through the practical activity of gesture, bodily signification and the conjuring of ethnic and cultural associations in rap performances. Within this grassroots rap culture, translocal identifications are performed through the use and reuse of rap lyrics and music videos produced in other towns and cities, as well as through young people's construction of imaginary relations with rappers from those places.

Disclosure statement

No potential conflict of interest was reported by the authors.

Funding

This work was supported by the Arts and Humanities Research Council [grant number AH/M011275].

ORCID

Richard Bramwell ⓘ http://orcid.org/0000-0002-3411-5223

References

Anderson, B. 1991. *Imagined Communities: Reflections on the Origin and Spread of Nationalism*. London: Verso.

Appadurai, A. 1996. *Modernity at Large: Cultural Dimensions of Globalization*. Minneapolis: University of Minnesota Press.

Back, L. 1988. "Coughing Up Fire: Soundsystems in South-East London." *New Formations*.

Baker, H. 1996. "Critical Memory and the Black Public Sphere." In *The Black Public Sphere*, 7–37. Chicago, IL: University of Chicago Press.

Bennett, A. 1999a. "Rappin' on the Tyne: White Hip Hop Culture in Northeast England – An Ethnographic Study." *The Sociological Review* 47 (1): 1–24.

Bennett, A. 1999b. "Hip Hop am Main: The Localization of Rap Music and Hip Hop Culture." *Media, Culture and Society* 21 (1): 77–91.

Bradley, L. 2013. *Sounds Like London: 100 Years of Black Music in the Capital*. London: Serpent's Tail.

Bramwell, R. 2015. *UK Hip Hop, Grime and the City: The Aesthetics and Ethics of London's Rap Scenes*. London: Routledge.

Bramwell, R. 2018. "Freedom Within Bars: Maximum Security Prisoners' Negotiations of Identity Through Rap." *Identities* 25 (4): 475–492.

Brickell, K., and A. Datta, eds. 2011. "Introduction: Translocal Geographies." In *Translocal Geographies: Spaces, Places, Connections*, 3–20. Farnham: Ashgate.

Chang, J. 2005. *Can't Stop, Won't Stop: A History of the Hip-Hop Generation*. London: Ebury Press.

Charles, M. 2018. "Grime Labour." *Soundings* 68: 40–52.

Condry, I. 2006. *Hip-Hop Japan: Rap and the Paths of Cultural Globalization*. Durham, NC: Duke University Press.

Darling-Wolf, F. 2008. "Getting Over Our 'Illusion D'Optique': From Globalization to Mondialisation (Through French Rap)." *Communication Theory* 18: 187–209.

Dedman, T. 2011. "Agency in UK Hip-Hop and Grime Youth Subcultures: Peripherals and Purists." *Journal of Youth Studies* 14 (5): 507–522.

Elafros, A. 2013. "Greek Hip Hop: Local and Translocal Authentication in the Restricted Field of Production." *Poetics* 41: 75–95.

Englert, B. 2018. "Looking Through Two Lenses: Reflections on Transnational and Translocal Dimensions in Marseille-Based Popular Music Relating to the Comoros." *Identities* 25 (5): 542–557.

Forman, M. 2000 "'Represent': Race, Space and Place in Rap Music." *Popular Music* 19 (1): 65–90.

Gilroy, P. 1987. *There Ain't No Black in the Union Jack: The Cultural Politics of Race and Nation*. London: Unwin Hyman.

Gilroy, P. 1991. "Sounds Authentic: Black Music, Ethnicity and the Challenge of a 'Changing' Same." *Black Music Research Journal* 11 (2): 111–136.

Gilroy, P. 1993. *The Black Atlantic*. London: Verso.

Gilroy, P. 2004. *After Empire: Melancholia or Convivial Culture?: Multiculture or Postcolonial Melancholia*. Oxon: Routledge.

Greiner, C., and P. Sakdapolrak. 2013. "Translocality: Concepts, Applications and Emerging Research Perspectives." *Geography Compass* 7 (5): 373–384.

Hall, S. 1995. "New Ethnicities." In *The Post-Colonial Studies Reader*, edited by Bill Ashcroft, Gareth Griffiths, and Helen Tiffin, 223–227. London: Routledge.

Hancox, D. 2018. *Inner City Pressure*. London: William Collins.

Heathcott, J. 2003. "Urban Spaces and Working-Class Expressions Across the Black Atlantic: Tracing the Routes of Ska." *Radical History Review* 87: 183–206.

Hesmondhalgh, D., and C. Melville. 2001. "Urban Breakbeat Culture." In *Global Noise*, edited by Tony Mitchell, 86–110. Middletown, CT: Weslyan University Press.

Hoyler, M., and C. Mager. 2005. "HipHop ist im Haus: Cultural Policy, Community Centres, and the Making of Hip-Hop Music in Germany." *Built Environment* 31 (3): 237–254.

Hunt, T. 2016. "Labour Must Embrace Englishness – And Be Proud of It." *The Guardian*. https://www.theguardian.com/commentisfree/2016/feb/05/labour-embrace-englishness-proud-patriotism.

James, M. 2015. *Urban Multiculture: Youth, Politics and Cultural Transformation in a Global City*. Basingstoke: Palgrave Macmillan.

Johnson, L. K. 1976. "Jamaican Rebel Music." *Race & Class* 17: 397–412.

Jones, R. 2018. "Music, Politics and Identity: From Cool Britannia to Grime4Corbyn." *Soundings* 67: 50–61.

Kajikawa, L. 2015. *Sounding Race in Rap Songs*. Oakland: University of California Press.

Ma, E. 2002. "Translocal Spatiality." *International Journal of Cultural Studies* 5: 131–152.

Major, J. 1993. "Speech to Conservative Group for Europe." http://www.johnmajor.co.uk/page1086.html.

Mitchell, T., ed. 2001. *Global Noise: Rap and Hip-Hop Outside the USA*. Middletown, CT: Weslyan University Press.

Nitzsche, S., and W. Grünzweig, eds. 2013. *Hip-Hop in Europe: Cultural Identities and Transnational Flows*. Berlin: LIT Verlag.

Noys, B. 1995. "Into the 'Jungle'." *Popular Music* 14 (3): 321–332.

Perkins, W. 1996. *Droppin Science: Critical Essays on Rap Music and Hip Hop Culture*. Philadelphia, PA: Temple University Press.

Rose, T. 1994. *Black Noise*. Middletown, CT: Weslyan University Press.

Scruton, R. 2016. "Who Are We?" *Prospect Magazine*.

Smith, M. 2011. "Translocality: A Critical Reflection." In *Translocal Geographies: Spaces, Places, Connections*, edited by K. Brickell and A. Datta, 181–198. Farnham: Ashgate.

Thapar, C. 2017. "From Chicago to Brixton: The Surprising Rise of UK Drill." https://www.factmag.com/2017/04/27/uk-drill-chicago-brixton/.

Turner, P. 2017. *Hip Hop Versus Rap: The Politics of Droppin' Knowledge*. London: Routledge.

White, J. 2016. *Urban Music and Entrepreneurship: Beats, Rhymes and Young People's Enterprise*. London: Routledge.

White, J. 2017. "Controlling the Flow: How Urban Music Videos Allow Creative Scope and Permit Social Restriction." *Young* 25 (4): 407–425.

Index

Abbott, Diane 50
Abedi, Salman 62
Afghan refugees 69, 79, 83, 90
Afghanistan, anti-Muslim racism 86
aid: development 13; humanitarian 65
Alexander, Claire 24
Anderson, Bridget 22
antiracism 23, 36, 44, 53; British values
    45–49; Cox, Brendan 47; Cox, Jo 52;
    ECHR 2; populism 8, 99, 101, 102,
    104–113
anti-semitism 50, 68
Anti-Terrorism Crime and Security Act
    (2001) 63
Appadurai, Arjun 120, 123
Arendt, H. 4, 66
asylum seekers: Labour Party policy 43;
    racial biopolitics 60; racist violence
    against 33; "refugee crisis" 90, 92;
    rights 69; as terror suspects 62, 63, 72;
    "undeserving" 70
Australian overstayers 33
authoritarian populism 10

Back, Les 122
Balibar, E. 25, 79
Benjamin, Walter 81
Bennett, A. 119
Bennism 17–18n8
Berger, Luciana 50
Bhabha, H. K. 81
Blairism 4
border/bordering 5–8, 9–10, 22; Brexit
    vote 61, 99–100; capitalism 15; in
    ethnic and racial studies 26–27; Gothic
    preoccupation with 68; multi-status
    Britain 25; neoliberalism 13; racism 33,
    34, 35–36; "refugee crisis" 78
Breaking Point poster 17n4, 49, 67–69,
    72, 99–100

Brexit 1; authoritarian populism 10;
    Breaking Point poster 17n4, 49,
    67–69, 72, 99–100; brinkmanship 15;
    capitalism 13, 15; class composition
    of vote 16, 104; Cox's assassination 39,
    40, 49, 53; Englishness 131; framing of
    referendum 2, 17n4; free movement
    issue 4, 16; illegal immigrants
    36n2; populism 98–104, 105–108,
    111–112, 113; Syrian "refugee crisis"
    60–63, 70, 71
Brickell, K. 119–120
Britain First 49, 61
British Cultural Studies 9
British values 42, 45–49, 52, 64
Brown, Gordon 112
Burnham, Andy 102–103

Cameron, David 14, 102
capitalism 10–14, 15, 16–17, 94
care, and the "refugee crisis" 78–95
Carter, D. 29
Casas-Cortes, M. 25
Casey Review (2016) 4
Charles, Monique 132
Chios 79–95
Choudhury, T. 64
citizenship 28; border in ethnic and racial
    studies 26, 27; capitalism 15; criminals
    27; Muslims as conditional citizens
    63–64; racism 31, 33, 34–35
civility 82
Clarke, Charles 73n1
class issues: capitalism 10; deportation
    30; racism 30, 71; Syrian refugees 70,
    71; see also middle class; working class
Clover, J. 17n5
coalition government 113
Cobain, I. 41
Collyer, M. 66

Cologne attacks 62, 69, 88
colonialism *see* imperialism and colonialism
concentration camps 59
concentrationary universe 58–59
Concentrationary Gothic 59–60, 62, 63–65, 67–69, 71–73
Conservative Party: Brexit 16, 102; British values 45; integrationist measures 4; neoliberalism 82, 113; populism 99, 102, 103, 106, 108; *see also* Cameron, David; Johnson, Boris; Major, John; May, Theresa; Thatcher, Margaret; Thatcherism
Cooper, Rosie 50
Corbyn, Jeremy 50, 103, 109
Counter-Terrorism and Security Act (2015) 63
Cox, Brendan 40, 46–47, 49, 51
Cox, Jo 6, 39–42, 45, 46–53, 61
criminal justice system: Cox's assassination 52; deportation 22, 27, 29–32, 33; Operation Nexus 34; racism 22, 29–34, 35–36, 112; rap 123; "refugee crisis", Greece 88, 90, 91, 92, 93, 94
cruelty, and the "refugee crisis" 78–95
cultural issues: backlash 2; capitalism 10, 11, 14; rap and hip hop 9, 118–133; Thatcherism 11, 12; *see also* multiculturalism

Daesh/Islamic State (IS) 62, 63, 65
Darling-Wolf, F. 120
Datta, A. 119–120
Davies, David 71
degeneration discourse 60
De Genova, N. 25
Denham, John 130
Denmark, populism 17n7
Department for International Development 40
deportation 15, 63, 22, 23, 27–36
development aid 13
diversity 2, 24, 25, 39, 101; *see also* multiculturalism
domestication 43–45; Cox's assassination 46–47, 51–52; of misogynist white supremacy 41–42, 49, 52–53
domopolitics 42, 43, 47, 50, 52
drill 122–123, 127, 128
Duncan Smith, Iain 13

economic restructuring 1, 2
Elafros, A. 120

electoral map 4
Englert, Birgit 120–121
Erel, U. 23
ethnic and racial studies, border within 26–27
European Central Bank 79
European Commission 65, 79, 88
European Convention on Human Rights (ECHR) 2, 17n3, 63
European Council 81, 93
European Union: capitalism 13; free movement 2, 4, 16; "postcolonial melancholia" 16; Thatcherism 11; *see also* Brexit

family reunification 4, 60
Fanon, F. 67, 71
Farage, Nigel: *Breaking Point* poster 17n4, 49, 67, 99–100; media coverage 114n3; Muslim women's abuse 45; populism 99–101, 103, 105–106, 107–108
Fassin, Eric 110
fertility 43
"folk devils" 10, 11
Forman, Murray 124
"Fortress Europe" 7, 70
France: Calais "Jungle" camp 60, 69, 70, 100; left nationalism 17n7; populism 98, 110; rap 120–121
Frederiksen, Mette 17n7
FRONTEX 85, 88, 90
Front National 98

gender issues: Cox's assassination 46–47; domestication 43; women's abuse 45–46; *see also* misogyny
Gentleman, Amelia 21
Germany: "Aufstehen" initiative 17n7; Cologne attacks 62, 69, 88; concentration camps 59; youth and community centres 125
Gibney, Matthew 33
Gilroy, Paul 14, 15, 17–18n8, 26, 66, 110, 119, 124–125, 129
Goldberg, D. T. 65, 67–68
Goodhart, David 102
Gramsci, A. 15
Gray, J. 11–12
Great Get Together 40, 47–49, 52
Greece: austerity 79, 86; hip hop 120; population exchange (1923) 84–85; populism 98; "refugee crisis" 79–95
Greiner, C. 119
grime 119, 121–122, 126, 131–132

Hage, Ghassan 41–42, 43–45, 52, 53, 61
Halberstam, J. 68, 71
Hall, Stuart 10, 11, 12, 14, 23, 110
Hardt, M. 14
Hesmondhalgh, D. 119, 122
hip hop 118–122, 131, 132
Hong Kong, hip hop 120
Hope Not Hate 46
Hotspot Programme 92
Hoyler, M. 125
human capital 13
humanitarian aid 65
humanitarianism 82
human rights: cruelty, elimination of 80; "Muslim question" 59; "refugee crisis" 58, 60, 65, 66, 67, 68, 70–71, 88, 89
Hunt, Tristram 130
Hurley, K. 71

identity politics 103
Iglesias, Pablo 98
illegal immigrants: deportation 22, 27, 29–31, 32–34; hostile environment 21, 36n1; race in migration studies 24–25; Windrush scandal 21–22
immigrants/immigration: Brexit 2, 49, 60–61, 99–101, 104, 106–107; British values 10; capitalism 10, 12, 14, 15; hostile environment 4, 21, 25, 36n1; left nationalism 8; neoliberalism 13; populism 8, 99–107, 112–113; portrayals of 4; "postcolonial melancholia" 16; race in migration studies 23–25; racism 22; rap 120, 121; Thatcherism 11; welfare access 4; see also asylum seekers; illegal immigrants; refugees
Immigration Act (2016) 60
Immigration, Asylum and Nationality Act (2006) 63
imperialism and colonialism 5, 14–16; Concentrationary Gothic 58–59; cruelty and care 80–82, 87, 89–90, 92–94; domestication 44; populism 110; race in migration studies 23–24; subjection and exclusion logics 67, 68; Syrian refugees 71
inclusion 44
integration 4; British values 45; Muslim refugees 61, 62; race in migration studies 23–24
International Monetary Fund 79
Iranian refugees 83, 90
Iraq 86
Iraqi refugees 79, 83, 90

Islam see Muslims
Islamic State (IS)/Daesh 62, 63, 65
Islamophobia 44, 61, 68, 112

Jamaica: deportation to 22, 27–36; music 121, 122
James, Malcolm 103
Jews 50, 67, 68
Jo Cox Foundation 46
Johnson, Boris 100
Jones, R. 132
"Jungle" camp, Calais 60, 69, 70, 100

Kaltwasser, Cristóbal Robira 111
Kaufmann, Eric 102
Khan, Sadiq 50
Khiari, Sadri 110
Kinnock, Stephen 103
Kirtsoglou, E. 65
Kurdi, Alan 87

Labour Party: Brexit 103; Cox's assassination 40, 43, 53; English identity 130; grime scene 132; Jo Cox Women in Leadership programme 40, 53; left nationalism 8; neoliberalism 113; populism 102–103, 104, 108, 112; social democracy and urban liberalism 2; *Strong Borders, Safe Haven* White Paper 42–43; white supremacist plots 50; see also Blairism; Corbyn, Jeremy; Cox, Jo
Laclau, Ernesto 99, 104–105, 106, 107, 109–110, 111, 113n2
left nationalism 8
Lentin, A. 23
Le Pen, Marie 98, 114n4
Lexiters 16
liberal elite: Muslim refugees 70; populism 99, 100–101, 102, 103, 104, 108, 109, 112
Little Englander nationalism 11, 16
Lonergan, Gwyneth 43

Ma, Eric 120
Macron, Emmanuel 114n4
Mager, C. 125
Mair, Thomas 39, 40–41, 45, 49–52, 53, 61
Major, John 130
Marxism 17
May, Theresa 36n1, 102, 103, 106
McGeever, B. 16
McKean, Benjamin 110
media culture 2
Mélenchon, Jean-Luc 17n7, 110

INDEX

Melville, C. 119, 122
Mexico, populism 111
middle class 16, 104
Mighall, R. 59
migrants *see* immigrants/immigration
migration studies, race in 23–26
military, Greek 93, 94
misogyny 46, 47, 50; Cox's assassination
41–42, 45, 53; domestication of 41–42,
49, 52–53
Mondon, Aurélien 103
Mooten, N. 87
More in Common 40, 42, 43, 45,
47–48, 52–53
Mouffe, Chantal 105, 107, 110, 111
Muddle, Cas 110–111
Müller, Jan-Werner 107
multiculturalism: Brexit referendum
campaign 2; domestication 44; liberal
elite 101; "Muslim question" 61;
neoliberalism 110; rap 9; working class
101, 109; *see also* diversity
multi-status Britain 25–26, 34, 35
Murji, K. 23
"Muslim question" 61, 62, 69
Muslims: alien cultures 5; capitalism
15; concentrationary gothic 7; as
conditional citizens 63–64; Khan,
Sadiq 50; populism 112; portrayals of
4; refugees 59–73; terror suspects 86;
Turkey's prospect of acceding to EU 2;
white supremacism 41, 44; women's
abuse 45–46

Nagle, A. 8
Nahaboo, Z. 23
National Action 50
Nayak, Anoop 35
Nazism 59, 81; Mair 39, 41; neo- 50;
propaganda video 68, 72
Negri, A. 14
neo-colonialism 67, 72
neoliberalism 15, 29; and capitalism 10,
11, 13–14; care 82; free movement
issue 16; and populism 105, 107, 109,
110, 113; "refugee crisis" 79, 81, 94
Netherlands, populism 98

Obama, Barack 40
Orwell, George 102

Partij voor de Vrijheid 98
Parveen, N. 41
Peru, populism 111
Podemos 98, 114n5

police *see* criminal justice system
populism 8, 98–99, 102–104; antiracist 8,
99, 101, 102, 104–113; authoritarian 10;
Brexit 60, 99–102; Gothic 69; hostility
towards immigration 4; More in
Common 47; political logic of 104–109;
refugees as terror suspects 62
Powellism 18n8, 108
Prevention of Terrorism Act (2005) 73n1
Puar, J. R. 66
Pugliese, J. 66

race in migration studies 23–26
racism: anti-Muslim 86; Brexit 106–109;
class issues 30, 71; criminal justice
system 22, 29–34, 35–36, 112; cruelty
80; deportation 22, 23, 27, 33, 34; as
hate crime 112; immigration control
22, 27, 28, 33, 35–36; as other to British
values 42, 46, 47; populism 99–102,
106–109; "refugee crisis" 68, 89, 92, 94
Rajaram, P. K. 67
rap 9, 118–133
Rassemblement national 98, 114n4
Raynor, Angela 103
Refugee Convention (1951) 58
refugees 7; Brexit referendum 17n4,
49, 99–100; care and cruelty 78–95;
dehumanisation 5, 7, 71–73, 90;
discrediting of 7; left nationalism 8;
Muslim 59–73; numbers 78; Syrian 60,
64–72, 79, 83, 89–90, 99
Reker, Henriette 88
reproduction 43
reverse colonisation 60, 62, 67
Robinson, Tommy 112–113
Roma 2
Romanians 2
Rousset, D. 58
Rudd, Amber 21

Said, Edward 59
Sakdapolrak, P. 119
Sales, R. 70
Scruton, Roger 130
sexism, as other to British values
42, 46
Slovakia 64
Smith, M. 120
Somalian refugees 79
Spain, populism 98, 114n5
Spurr, D. 71
Stalinism 81
student visas 4
superdiversity 24, 25

140   INDEX

Syria, anti-Muslim racism 86
Syrian refugees 60, 64–72, 79, 83, 89–90, 99
Syriza 98

Taylor, M. 41
Tell MAMA 61
terror suspects, Muslim refugees
   conflated with 61–72
Terrorism Act (2006) 63
Thatcher, Margaret 10, 11, 12
Thatcherism 10, 11–12, 14, 16
Thornberry, Emily 112
translocality 119–121, 123, 125–127, 129,
   132–133
Trump, Donald 47, 98
Tsimouris, E. 65
Tsipras, Alexis 98
TUC 61
Turkey, prospect of accession to EU 2

UK Independence Party (UKIP): Cox's
   assassination 49; media coverage
   114n3; populism 99, 102, 103,
   105–106, 107; *see also* Farage, Nigel
Ukrainian refugees 79
United Nations High Commissioner for
   Refugees (UNHCR) 62, 66, 78, 85, 89
United States: hip hop 118–119, 120, 121,
   122, 131; populism 98; state-building
   47

Valluvan, Sivamohan 103
Venezuela, populism 111
Vertovec, Steven 24, 25
Virdee, S. 16
Vulnerable Persons Relocation Scheme
   (VPRS) 60, 62, 64, 65–66, 72

Wacquant, L. 29
Wagenknecht, Sahra 17n7
Wagner, C. 69
Walters, William 42–43, 46, 52
war on terror 59, 62–66, 85
welfare state: capitalism 16; care 82; and
   citizenship status 29; left nationalism 8;
   populism 103
White Pendragons 50
white supremacism 44–45, 46, 47, 50;
   Cox's assassination 39, 40–42, 45, 46,
   53; domestication of 41–42, 49,
   52–53
Wilders, Geert 98
Windrush scandal 21–22
Winter, Aaron 103
working class: Brexit 16, 104; capitalism
   10; "deservingness" 16; "grime
   generation" 132; left nationalism 8;
   populism 99, 100–101, 102, 103, 104,
   109; Syrian refugees 70, 71
work-permits 4
World Trade Organization (WTO) 15